Gina

X-chromosomes within The X-Files

Gina Boyer Rumbaugh

X-chromosomes within The X-Files

An Examination of Celebrity Role Models Agent Scully and Gillian Anderson

VDM Verlag Dr. Müller

Impressum/Imprint (nur für Deutschland/ only for Germany)
Bibliografische Information der Deutschen Nationalbibliothek: Die Deutsche Nationalbibliothek verzeichnet diese Publikation in der Deutschen Nationalbibliografie; detaillierte bibliografische Daten sind im Internet über http://dnb.d-nb.de abrufbar.

Coverbild: www.purestockx.com

Verlag: VDM Verlag Dr. Müller Aktiengesellschaft & Co. KG
Dudweiler Landstr. 125 a, 66123 Saarbrücken, Deutschland
Telefon +49 681 9100-698, Telefax +49 681 9100-988, Email: info@vdm-verlag.de

Herstellung in Deutschland:
Schaltungsdienst Lange o.H.G., Zehrensdorfer Str. 11, D-12277 Berlin
Books on Demand GmbH, Gutenbergring 53, D-22848 Norderstedt
Reha GmbH, Dudweiler Landstr. 99, D- 66123 Saarbrücken
ISBN: **978-3-639-07196-2**

Imprint (only for USA, GB)
Bibliographic information published by the Deutsche Nationalbibliothek: The Deutsche Nationalbibliothek lists this publication in the Deutsche Nationalbibliografie; detailed bibliographic data are available in the Internet at http://dnb.d-nb.de.

Cover image: www.purestockx.com

Publisher:
VDM Verlag Dr. Müller Aktiengesellschaft & Co. KG
Dudweiler Landstr. 125 a, 66123 Saarbrücken, Germany
Phone +49 681 9100-698, Fax +49 681 9100-988, Email: info@vdm-verlag.de

Produced in USA and UK by:
Lightning Source Inc., 1246 Heil Quaker Blvd., La Vergne, TN 37086, USA
Lightning Source UK Ltd., Chapter House, Pitfield, Kiln Farm, Milton Keynes, MK11 3LW, GB
BookSurge, 7290 B. Investment Drive, North Charleston, SC 29418, USA
ISBN: **978-3-639-07196-2**

ACKNOWLEDGEMENTS

I am extremely privileged to have studied under and alongside the members of my graduate committee, Professors Leslie Steeves, Carl Bybee, and Kim Sheehan. To Leslie, my advisor, I am especially grateful for the valuable direction and unwavering encouragement she provided throughout the several years it took to complete this project. To Carl, I am eternally indebted for introducing me to cultural studies and the joy of qualitative research. To Kim, I owe special thanks for her enthusiasm to review my work from a fresh perspective. I also extend sincere gratitude to my friend and peer, Randy Nichols, who assured me countless times that I could do it. Finally, to my husband, Christopher, I give my deepest thanks for his patience and support as I worked to fulfill a dream.

TABLE OF CONTENTS

CHAPTER I

INTRODUCTION

In 2002, the National Organization for Women's *Feminist Primetime Report* rated the network television series *The X-Files* an A+ for its depiction of women "as active participants in the plot, as intelligent and skilled human beings in charge of their own lives," and who were "treated with respect" (p. 13). Since Special Agent Dana Scully is the only leading woman character on *The X-Files*, it is she, specifically, to whom this rating of A+ applies. After nine broadcast seasons and 202 episodes, 2002 also marked the final year in which *The X-Files* was produced. The show's reputation for presenting a strong female character was not a recent development, though. From the time the series debuted in 1993 and up through its last season, Scully was consistently lauded as a role model for girls and women.

The cultural significance of the Scully character is profound in regard to contemporary television images of women, wherein she has been called "the main inspiration for a whole generation of pop-culture heroines" (Strauss, 2001, Revitalized section, para. 1). The framing of Scully as a role model calls for a closer examination of how and why she came to symbolize the best of 1990s television in terms of women characters. It furthermore encompasses the influence that Gillian Anderson, the actor who played Scully, has had on fan practices of identification and imitation. The dual star images of Scully and Gillian Anderson converged to produce a female role model that inspired an extensive female fan following and, through fan activity, ultimately generated hundreds of thousands of dollars for nonprofit organizations.

The various components related to the leading female character in *The X-Files* – text, context, star, and fans – amount to a unified and dynamic cultural construct. While feminist scholars commonly and successfully consider such elements independent of each other, I believe that a holistic approach can bring about a deeper understanding of the cultural mechanisms surrounding mediated images of women and their effect on women viewers. Toward qualitative knowledge of popular culture, role modeling, and women, I examine *The X-Files* textual incarnation of the Scully character, popular press discourse on the merits of Scully and Gillian Anderson, the real person of Gillian Anderson, and online fan activity.

"If you write about [celebrity] you are obliged to come to terms with the ways in which you think it may have affected your own sense of reality – declare your interest, as it were, to the degree that you can determine what it is" (Schickel, 1985, p. 65). As a regular viewer of *The X-Files*, I would oftentimes read popular magazine articles about the show and its stars, as well as peruse fan websites for news updates and public bulletin boards for critical analysis. In short, I was (and still am) a fan. Indeed, "We are all fans of something" (Lewis, 1992, p. 1). Cultural critic Lawrence Grossberg (1992) similarly asserts, "everyone is constantly a fan of various sorts of things, for one cannot exist in a world where nothing matters..." (p. 63). And, because we live in a world where things *do* matter – where culture matters – we naturally develop personal attachments to what we deem significant. We are fans of particular people and practices that cause us to reflect on ourselves and, consequently, shape our identity. As we continually construct and modify our own unique cultural "mattering maps," we learn from what surrounds us, inevitably incorporating aspects of myriad influences into our character. Fandom is a visible manifestation of that which matters to us and of who we may strive to emulate at different points during our lives. This concept is helpful to recognize because it is by "endeavoring to understand the fan impulse" that we "ultimately move towards a greater understanding of ourselves" (Lewis, 1992, p. 1). Through this research project, I have gained understanding into the workings of popular culture – as it affects both fans and the famous. I have also gained insight into my own identity as a fan, particularly in my effort to reconcile the noble principles of academic scholarship with my personal motives for studying a subject, *The X-Files*, of which I am fond. I eventually determined that being a fan of a popular culture artifact need not distract from a fair theoretical treatment of it; rather, my knowledge of the topic has proven immensely beneficial to my study. It is precisely *because* I respect *The X-Files* and its fandom that I worked so diligently to interpret the ways in which the series, Scully, and Gillian Anderson influence people's lives.

The entertainment I derived as a weekly viewer of *The X-Files* evolved into a desire to examine it from an academic perspective, of which there exists a substantial amount of published material. What I found are largely textually-based ideological analyses that, while interesting and illuminating, nonetheless lack discussion of certain pleasurable aspects of the series, foremost concerning Scully as a positive female role model. Instead, the analyses tend to emphasize the many personal tragedies Scully suffered during her tenure as a FBI agent, including multiple abductions (by aliens, government operatives, and criminals), blocked memory, forced sterility, and cancer. Such destructive renderings of Scully's female body have reasonably led to feminist critiques delineating the stereotypic patriarchal values presented in *The X-Files*. Most of what is written has emerged from the more sophisticated theoretical tradition that filmic depictions of women are defined by and intended for the pleasure of male characters, male directors, and male audiences. If female characters are to function as passive images to the male gaze, as Scully has been shown to do, little room is left for female viewers to engage in authentic identification with those female characters. Overall, the analyses seem to suggest that appreciation of or identification with the positive attributes of Scully is futile.

While seeking to integrate my enjoyment of *The X-Files* series and of the Scully character with the valid arguments put forth by feminist scholars on the subject, I was heartened to come across Jackie Stacey's (1994) remarks pertaining to research on representations of women: "Following Laura Mulvey's original attack on the visual pleasure of narrative cinema, such feminist work on the process of identification is still marked by a suspicion of any kind of feminine role model, heroine or image of identification" (p. 132). This continuing suspicion about role model research and the types of rudimentary analyses it produced primarily during the 1970s has inevitably diminished its likelihood of a resurgence in feminist media studies. But, as Stacey examines in her study of fans and stars, and Caughey (1984) in his volume on imaginary social relationships, processes of identification and role modeling remain ubiquitous practices among the viewing public and should not be disregarded as a habit of the less informed. Women glean significant benefit from watching other women (in real and fictional settings) face challenges and prevail. Specific to *The X-Files*, they are inspired by the positive image of Scully and, by extension, Gillian Anderson, at times appropriating her/their behavior in order to manage their own personal and professional issues. The vast majority of online fan discourse about Scully and Gillian Anderson is expressive of the encouragement that women receive from these two celebrated images. Beyond talk, practices of imitative behavior offer additional avenues for fans to express admiration for their idol, at times to the benefit of charitable entities external to *X-Files* fandom. All of this activity obligates a theoretically and methodologically balanced treatment of the cultural implications of Scully and Gillian Anderson as positive female role models.

My aim in writing about the women of *The X-Files* – Scully and Gillian Anderson – and about how women viewers negotiate these two star images toward discovering spaces of identification and imitation is to begin to fill what I perceive to be a gap in the scholarship on this culturally resonant media text. In the process, I hope to demonstrate the efficacy of role model research in contemporary feminist media studies. Broadly, I accomplish this by employing a qualitative framework delimited by analytical practices of feminist cultural studies. This project is built on the set of assumptions that, 1) cultural products emanate from a dominant frame of reference that privileges male voices and experiences over female interests, 2) media texts are ideologically encoded to sustain these dominant values, but polysemic to the extent that they can be "restructured in preference for alternative readings" (Gledhill, 1988, p. 74), and 3) a feminist treatment of the subject matter can illuminate spaces of authentic female identification and agency. As is common to qualitative endeavors, the research questions addressed in this study are both descriptive and analytic in nature, and are discussed in terms of my preferred theoretical perspectives as a researcher and my personal perceptions as a woman. They focus on the construction, or framing, of Scully and Gillian Anderson as role models, and on how female fans and Gillian Anderson herself negotiate their positions within the role model construct. The issues are explored through several interpretive research strategies, including textual analysis of the Scully character within *The X-Files* television series, historical treatment of popular press discourse on Gillian Anderson, an in-depth interview with Gillian Anderson supplemented by press interviews, and analysis of tertiary texts and activity created and performed by fans.

I begin by devoting Chapter Two to a review of the contextual framework of *The X-Files* – moving from a general summary of the television landscape on to which the series emerged in 1993, to discussions of corporate and creative aspects of the show and its cultural resonance in the age of the Internet, and concluding with accounts of Scully the character and Gillian Anderson the actor. Chapter Three is the review of literature, incorporating feminist media theory on images of women, woman as image, and the concept of negotiation; fan-star theory on para-social relationships and identification processes; scholarship on *The X-Files*; and an explanation of the research questions. This is followed by a description in Chapter Four of the integrated methodology specifically developed for examining the subject, the limitations of the study, and the structure of the analysis chapters that follow. Chapter Five addresses how Scully via the text and Gillian Anderson via the popular press are constructed as role models for women, while Chapter Six considers the negotiation processes of Gillian Anderson as a role model and of female fans in their efforts to identify with that role model. Chapter Seven concludes the critique.

In order to credibly determine whether *The X-Files* warrants its rating of A+ for what it offers in terms of television portrayals of women, I defer to those who frame and negotiate those portrayals to provide the answer – Scully, the popular press, Gillian Anderson, and fans.

CHAPTER II

CONTEXTUAL FRAMEWORK

Television Landscape: From Backlash to Quality

Prime-time television was in transition when *The X-Files* made its debut in the early 1990s. The decade before had been a period in broadcast history described by Susan Faludi (1991) as a cultural "backlash" that "succeeded in depopulating TV of its healthy independent women and replacing them with nostalgia-glazed portraits of apolitical 'family' women" (p. 148). Fueled by Reagan-era conservatism of the 1980s, this backlash was exemplified by lead female characters' "disappearance from prime-time [network] television" (p. 143). Devaluation of the self-reliant single woman recently celebrated in television programs of the 1970s was most obvious in situation comedies. Series featuring progressive ideals like *The Mary Tyler Moore Show* and *One Day at a Time* had been replaced by "family" fare such as *The Cosby Show* and *Family Ties*, in which the wife-mother's professional career was neglected narratively in favor of her primary role of caregiver. Also produced during this period were prime-time dramas featuring educated female characters, ostensibly as co-leads to male characters. Examples of popular programs with a male-female detective partner premise not unlike *The X-Files* include *Hart to Hart, Scarecrow and Mrs. King, Moonlighting*, and *Remington Steele*. However, in these and other shows with co-lead scenarios, narratives featuring the women were oftentimes disregarded in deference to stories about the men, consequently relegating female leads to supportive role stereotypes.

Flawed as they may have been in terms of gender parity, several shows of the 1980s managed to make women relevant in a television landscape teeming with testosterone where the likes of *Miami Vice, Knight Rider, A-Team, MacGyver*, and *Magnum P.I.* left little room for women to flourish. Indeed, television did present a few strong female protagonists during the decade, most notably in situation comedies *Murphy Brown* and *Roseanne*, and in women-centered dramatic series

Cagney & Lacey, *Sisters*, and *China Beach*. These noteworthy dramas were part of a rising programming trend called "quality television," which helped establish that female-oriented television could be commercially viable.

Quality television is a style of programming with an aesthetic that incorporates independent authorship, sophisticated storytelling, nontraditional narrative, cultural reflexivity, and a proclivity for "realism" (Thompson, 1996, pp. 15, 192). The coalescence of artistic excellence with an affluent audience base usually produce shows that receive high critical acclaim. During the 1980s, many quality programs also resonated strongly with women viewers, especially at a time when so few female role models were made available in broadcast media. However, shortly after the turn of the decade, media watchers proclaimed that quality television had already begun to decline: "By the 1993-94 season, critics, insiders, and prognosticators all across the country had declared the death...of the quality drama" (p. 179). With enthusiasm for a programming style that often emphasized strong female characters allegedly waning, progress made toward counteracting the backlash of 1980s broadcasting could have been in jeopardy of stalling. Amidst the uncertainty, writers and producers remained interested in the ideal of quality television and it endured. When *The X-Files* pilot was produced in 1993, prime-time dramas that offered both quality *and* featured women in lead roles were showing signs of emerging as a profitable programming strategy. Fortunately for the producers of *The X-Files*, the television industry was rapidly transitioning to capitalize on this trend.

The X-Files 101: Corporate and Creative Considerations

Commercial Factors, Genre, and Narrative

In view of the generally conservative nature of television network programming, *The X-Files* was a risky concept. Essentially, it is about two people – FBI special agents Dana Scully and Fox Mulder – in search of the "truth." Operating from this simple but intriguing premise, the program's appeal is realized through mysteries involving secret governments, alien existence, and bizarre phenomena investigated jointly by agents from opposite frames-of-reference. Agent Scully believes the truth is knowable only through the certainties of scientific rigor, while Agent Mulder believes the answers are "out there" in the supernatural realm. Together, they employ contradictory techniques of science and the paranormal to work toward uncovering the truth of unsolved cases labeled X-Files. The show's opening credits declare "The Truth is Out There." However, creator and executive producer Chris Carter adds the caveat, "the truth...is so far out there that we'll never find it" (Casimir, 1996, para. 29). Hence, the ongoing dramatic conflict of *The X-Files* – unlikely government partners, one woman and one man, committed to investigating outlandish cases in pursuit of an eternally elusive truth.

The X-Files was produced as a pilot in March 1993 and was considered along with 37 other concepts for FOX Broadcasting Company's fall television line-up (Lowry, 1995, p. 3). FOX was a young network struggling for market share in 1993 (the first year it aired programming all seven nights of the week), which made it well situated to experiment with unconventional programming. The broadcasting newcomer greenlighted programs unlikely to be found on the Big Three television networks in its bid to carve out a niche among viewers, and a show about alien abduction and government conspiracy fit its ambitious formula. *The X-Files* pilot proved successful and the show landed a trial run on Friday nights at 9:00 p.m. Though it picked up the series, FOX wasn't overly optimistic about its ratings potential. In fact, the network heavily focused promotional attention on the Friday night lead-in to *The X-Files* – a short-lived program called *The Adventures of Brisco County Jr.* (Wild, 1996, para. 2).

Needing to elect a primary vehicle through which to market *The X-Files*, network executives assigned the series to the science fiction genre, despite initial resistance from its creator ("The X-Files meets the skeptics," 1996). Carter envisioned a multi-faceted series that had substantial narrative potential, and which could not be limited by one generic label. By regularly weaving together a multitude of other genres outside its science fiction core such as detective, thriller, horror, action-adventure, melodrama, and even comedy, *The X-Files* defies narrow classification. According to cultural critic Lidia Curti (1998), "it would be difficult to name a genre, or a gender, or even consider [*The X-Files*] a variation of one" (p. 73). By employing a medley of generic elements set within the context of FBI cases, the series yields interesting and diverse stories that appeal to a broader audience than might be achieved through strictly science fiction storylines.

In addition to crossing genre borders, *The X-Files* operates along two narrative tracks – a serial story arc called the "Mythology" (constituting approximately 25% of the show's repertoire), and a standard series structure of discrete plots commonly referred to as "Monster-of-the-Week." The serial-based conspiracy through-story is featured intermittently during the course of each season, building upon events that were aired weeks, months, and even years earlier, while the more common series format of stand-alone episodes provides frequent opportunity for the introduction of fresh plots and characters. Amid these dual storytelling methods is also a self-contained film entitled *The X-Files: Fight the Future* (1998) which develops the continuing Mythology arc via conventional cinematic narrative.

Production Standards, Stories, and Characters

For its first five years, *The X-Files* filmed in Vancouver, British Columbia. Because it was less expensive to shoot in Canada than in Hollywood, producers were able to maximize their limited budget to create a high-quality stylized series. Carter notes their philosophy was to "make a little movie each week" (Spelling, 2000, June 17, para. 10). Filming in southwest Canada in winter could have effectively dampened this aspiration, but Carter used it to his advantage. Aided by the weather and imaginative cinematography, he infused *The X-Files* with an eerie flavor that complemented stories of strange happenings and government cover-ups. When production was moved to Southern California at the start of its sixth season, some of the show's signature gloom may have been lost, but Carter was by then able to command enough budget to maintain its film-like quality. Media critics took note of the exceptional elements inherent to *The X-Files*: "[T]he dialogue was crisp and wryly literature; the pacing was brilliant; and the camera work, virtually without distracting special effects, was as good as the best work of Spielberg (Close Encounters) or John Carpenter (Halloween)" (McConnell, 1994, p. 18); and "intelligent writing and sharp plotting lift the series far above the standard for the genre" (Pennington, 1993, p. 6G). Carter's creative authorship and nurture of the series throughout its nine-year run afforded *The X-Files* a consistently high level of quality and continuity.

The quality of *The X-Files* extends beyond its superior production standards, to its caliber of stories. Carter contends the nature of *The X-Files* series is plot-driven and that success of the show relies on its ability to tell good scary tales. His use of sophisticated storytelling (e.g., fusion of genres) and unconventional narrative (e.g., combination of serial and series formats, indefinite episode endings) are attributes of quality television that earned *The X-Files* a reputation early on of being "cerebral" television (Thompson, 1996, p. 185) that "smart adults can watch...without scoffing" (Grahnke, 1993, p. 61). It is a show that respects viewers for their intelligence and ability to understand narrative nuances. And, although writers other than Carter penned a majority of the 202 *X-Files* scripts, Carter steadfastly adhered to his requirement for exceptional stories. He maintained final authority over each episode by ensuring his was "always the last typewriter through which the teleplay passe[d]" (Lowry, 1996, p. 236). While acknowledging the importance of characters, Carter asserts that without the compelling stories there would be no *X-Files* (Spelling, 2000, September).

Still, it could be alternately argued that even with great stories there would be no *X-Files* without the *characters*. Certainly Agents Dana Scully and Fox Mulder are more popularly recognized than are individual plots of the series, particularly for their idiosyncratic relationship. The most distinguishing feature of the duo is that they embody role-reversed gender stereotypes. Carter deliberately wrote the woman as a skeptic who values science above other ways of knowing and the man as a believer who first follows his intuition ("The X-Files meets the skeptics," 1996). While neither these realms is wholly unique to male or female sensibilities, the stereotype exists that men tend toward a scientific dichotomy of true/false, while women are inclined to allow for various explanations of events. In reversing these labels, Carter belies audience expectations of how men and women should think and behave.

Another hallmark of Scully and Mulder is their faithfulness as friends, not lovers. Carter adamantly resisted television cliché by denying his lead characters a physical romance, claiming that such a development would effectively compromise the integrity of the show. Instead, Scully and Mulder share a bond of respect and trust between a woman and a man rare in television. By reversing gender roles and refusing the romantic norm, *The X-Files* turns attention away from any presumed male-female stereotypic dynamic and liberally treats its two principals as *co*-leads. Scully is permitted ample opportunity to argue the merits of Western scientific epistemology, while Mulder is likewise privileged to share about his supernatural experiences.

Cultural Resonance: Popularity and Connectivity

Popularity Among Audience, Press, and Peers

As an unusual new show airing Friday nights on a fledgling broadcast network, it is not surprising that *The X-Files* got off to a slow start in the Nielsens Ratings (Carmody, 1993, p. C8). However, by its second season, the series had sold broadcast rights in 56 countries and was winning its timeslot nationally among the coveted 18- to 49-year-old demographic (Kantrowitz and Rogers, 1994). In terms of audience size, *The X-Files* reached its pinnacle during the fifth season with an average of 19.8 million viewers tuning in for each episode, and was ostensibly considered "the most popular series on Earth" ("Great Expectations," 1999). Following five increasingly successful years, *The X-Files: Fight the Future* feature film release in the summer of 1998 grossed $185 million worldwide. The movie's success both domestically and abroad, coupled with a sizeable franchise that included the television series, DVDs, books, collectibles, computer games, and conventions, ultimately earned FOX in excess of $1 billion (Grossberg, 2001). Concurrent with the show's popularity came due recognition of its creator and executive producer when, in 1997, *Time* magazine labeled him an influential "televisionary" along the lines of Rod Serling and Gene Roddenberry ("The 25 Most Influential People in America," 1997).

A good deal of the popularity of *The X-Files* is owed to enthusiastic coverage of the series and its stars by the entertainment press. It rightly responded to viewers' mounting interest in the show, but, above that, members of the press also independently appreciated the uniqueness of the program. Early reviews were generally affirming: "Oddball X-Files pushes all the right buttons" (Quill, 1993,

p. D6); "The lead characters have a quirky chemistry that (refreshingly) isn't built on the 'squabble and kiss' standard" (Pennington, 1993, p. 6G); and, "This is some of the very best storytelling on the Tube these days" (McConnell, 1994, p. 18). A handful of critics judged otherwise, such as the reviewer who thought *The X-Files* was "stupid," "malarkey," and "ought to be the ex-series before very long" (Shales, 1993, p. G7); and another who found the popularity of the show "difficult to understand" (Grossberger, 1995, p. 30). But, by the time the series was renewed for a second season, press feedback was virtually all positive. *The X-Files* had swelled into a "massive cult phenomenon, a sober but trippy conspiracy a go-go" (Wild, 1996, para. 3) that neither the press nor the television industry could overlook.

 The X-Files' immense popularity resonated beyond viewers and critics, to the television industry itself. Honoring entities including the Emmys, Golden Globes, and Screen Actor's Guild recognized the series with over 60 nominations and awards in categories covering drama series, female actor, male actor, cinematography, writing, editing, art direction, make-up, music, sound, and directing. Other groups representing audience interests, namely Viewers for Quality Television and Parent's Choice Awards, also lauded the series for its excellence in broadcasting. Acknowledgements of *The X-Files'* import in popular culture include a place on the Viewers for Quality Television's list of the ten best dramas of the 1990s and a spread in Dan Epstein's volume on *20th Century Pop Culture* (2000).

 The trendy reputation of *The X-Files* is further reflected by the degree to which it is referenced by other 1990s popular culture artifacts. Itself a product of pop culture, *The X-Files* has been cited extensively in television programs, movies, books, songs, cartoons, comics, and advertisements. Venues range from daytime drama *All My Children's* lead diva Erica Kane asking why friends are "suddenly acting like Scully and Mulder," to a furry monster on *Sesame Street* playing *The X-Files* theme music on his xylophone. Other examples include mentions in books by Stephen King and Dean Koontz, M&M's candy characters investigating "The M Files," and *The New Yorker* magazine's send-up of Mulder and Scully looking into reports of Santa Claus. Even for non-viewers of the show, references to Scully and Mulder, or hearing *The X-Files* signature music, are familiar cues that something strange or conspiratorial is afoot.

Connectivity of X-Philes

Prior to being propelled to *pop* status, *The X-Files* first established a level of *cult* status not uncommon in quality television. However, as the history of quality dramas attests, staying on the air can be challenging even for shows with a vocal following. It is possible that, had *The X-Files* launched a few years earlier, it would have been cancelled before the end of its first season. Providentially, the show's debut in 1993 paralleled the proliferation of computer-mediated-communication via the Internet. What differentiated *The X-Files'* immense success from the 1980s quality programming that struggled for viability was general user accessibility to the World Wide Web through the first software browser, Mosaic. Mosaic enabled non-academic and non-government users the opportunity to easily navigate the expanding network of graphical information on the Internet. The ability of burgeoning *X-Files* fans to connect with each other through electronic bulletin boards and websites ignited the growth of "X-Phile" loyalists. Casual cultural critics across the country joined computer-literate academics online to analyze, debate, and support an entertainment rarity: intellectually stimulating television. Even producers took advantage of the new technology. Carter admits using the Internet to monitor fan reactions, though he denies going so far as to alter storylines to accommodate viewer criticisms or suggestions (Kantrowitz and Rogers, 1994; Wild, 1996). Achieving an immediate cult following linked virtually in cyberspace moreover afforded the show an identifiable viewership that could be marketed as both desirable and reachable to advertisers. Ellen Seiter (1999) writes, "The *X-Files* producers recognized the perfect synergy of its high demographic fans and the Internet, and targeted its audience through the World Wide Web, a move that helped both to prove its audience share to executives contemplating axing the show, and to generate more publicity for the program" (p. 119).

One of the most significant contributions of the Internet in regard to broadcast fare has been its facilitation of participatory fanship. Indeed, early success of *The X-Files* is due in large part to the rapid emergence of an online fan presence, from which a core group organized and pressured the studio to renew the series for a second season. Interaction among this committed electronic audience subculture was instrumental in building a viewer base and, subsequently, broader audience and secondary media interest in the program. As the number of *X-Files*-related websites and discussion forums grew exponentially, so also did attention to certain elements of the series – especially its stars. Scores of websites extolling the virtues of actors Gillian Anderson and David Duchovny, in addition to the characters they play, Dana Scully and Fox Mulder, are available to anyone with connectivity.

Many of the celebrity-focused websites offer the requisite collection of star text material, including biographical facts, news, rumors, and critique of the actors' "private" lives. Some, however, share more substantial information and avenues for fan involvement. Two notable websites dedicated to Gillian Anderson that have historically provided the means for fans to become involved in her favored causes are the Official Gillian Anderson Website (www.gilliananderson.ws/main.shtml) and Order of the Blessed Saint Scully the Enigmatic (www.obsse.com). Originated in 1996 and still actively maintained, the Official Gillian Anderson Website (GAWS) is authorized by Gillian Anderson to serve as her official website. As such, it gives considerable space to promoting the charities in which she is personally involved. In its endeavor to generate both awareness and funds, GAWS has hosted seven annual online auctions to benefit her primary charity, Neurofibromatosis, Inc. (NF). Order of the Blessed Saint Scully the Enigmatic, unique for its focus on the character of Scully, has honored Gillian Anderson by hosting annual "Scully Marathons" in which sponsors are enlisted to donate money to NF for participants to watch "Scully-centric" *X-Files* episodes. These are but two exemplary websites among dozens that have been created in homage to the female lead of *The X-Files*. They represent the power of virtual communities to connect people of diverse backgrounds, as well as demonstrate how fan participation in celebrity-endorsed charities can be successfully fostered via the Internet.

Scully the Character and Gillian Anderson the Actor

Scully

For most viewers, adoration of actors Gillian Anderson and David Duchovny generally follows initial admiration for their fictive counterparts, Agents Scully and Mulder. The two attractive principals of *The X-Files* offer refreshing interpretations of male-female partnerships and adeptly illustrate how friendship and profundity can make for entertaining television. As the show's creator, Chris Carter envisioned a layered leading female character in Special Agent Dana Scully. Inspired by Jodie Foster's rendition of a young female FBI recruit in *The Silence of the Lambs* (1991) (Gross and Miller, 2001), Carter crafted her as intelligent, serious, and compassionate – a positive image of a contemporary woman who is successful and respected working within a mostly male milieu. Scully is a forensic scientist and medical doctor who, brought up in the Catholic faith, is conflicted by her dual beliefs in science and religion. One visible symbol of this inner struggle is the cross necklace she always wears, a reminder to her and viewers alike of the inherent tension between knowledge and belief.

Another marker of Scully's complex character is found in Carter's choice of his female lead's surname. Scully is the namesake of former Los Angeles Dodgers announcer Vin Scully, a legendary figure who Carter regards metaphorically as the "voice of God" (Lowry, 1995, p. 11). Following Richard Dyer's (1979) contention that names "usually imply quite a lot about a character" (p. 109), the idea that Scully denotes God is consistent with Carter's construction of her throughout the series as the authoritative voice of "truth." A scientist trained in Western medicine, Scully's definition of truth is rooted in the natural world and based on whether phenomena can be proved through scientific methods either now or in the future. She tells Mulder: "Nothing happens in contradiction to nature, only in contradiction to what we know of it" ("Herrenvolk," original airdate October 4, 1996). As the purveyor of knowable truth, Scully's function in the narrative is to represent conventional wisdom. In contrast, the Mulder character works to undermine the absolutism of traditional science.

Scully and Mulder's differing beliefs are immediately established in the pilot episode. The story opens when, two years into her tenure, Scully is reassigned from a teaching position with the FBI Academy at Quantico to partner with Bureau outsider Agent Mulder. Upon their initial meeting, Mulder challenges Scully: "When convention and science offer us no answers, might we not finally turn to the fantastic as a plausibility?" To which Scully resolutely responds: "What I find fantastic is any notion that there are answers beyond the realm of science" ("The Pilot," original airdate September 10, 1993). From the start, and continuing for nine seasons, Scully articulates the value of scientific precedence and its fundamental role in solving cases. Furthermore, according to Carter (Lowman, 2000, para. 8), the show is essentially told from Scully's point of view. As the de facto narrator of *The X-Files*, Scully's reliance on science to make sense of the paranormal activity she and her partner encounter is intended to reflect the epistemological perspective of the audience. Mulder credits the supernatural while Scully calmly and consistently interjects her (and ostensibly the audience's) reliable voice of reason into the narrative.

The scriptwriting strategy of presenting contradictory perspectives was intended to equally privilege Scully and Mulder in their investigative assessments of events. However, Carter's vision inevitably evolved into a preference for one character over the other. He comments, "I wanted Agent Scully to be right as much as Agent Mulder. Lo and behold, those stories were really boring" ("The X-Files meets the skeptics," 1996, p. 27). Thus, the gaze of the audience is ultimately directed through Mulder since he is the one with whom viewers are sympathetically positioned to identify. As Gillian Anderson says, "The audience is on his side" (Denton, 1996). But while the show is effectively premised on Mulder's penchant for the paranormal, and his observations are accorded more authority, it is Scully who keeps the story grounded. She complements Mulder's idealistic notions with pragmatism and objectivity, bringing both she and her partner closer to the truth.

Gillian Anderson

Casting Scully was an arduous process. Carter sought someone who could portray Scully as earnest yet interesting; who could balance the character's sober demeanor with a sympathetic style and subtle wit; and who could play a scientist credibly. His determination to select a woman capable of conveying these central attributes led him to set a very high standard for auditioning actors. Having seen countless women prior to unknown stage actor Gillian Anderson, Carter recognized immediately that she embodied what he was looking for: "I knew the moment I met Gillian she was Scully. ... She had a seriousness for a young woman that I felt would work great for the character I imagined" (Lowman, 2000, para. 11). Her confidence and chemistry playing opposite David Duchovny solidified Carter's decision.

However, FOX executives were resistant to any deviation from their successful primetime formula of "bustier and leggier" female characters (ala *Melrose Place*), and insisted Carter see additional actors in the hopes he find a sexier woman. Backed by casting director Randy Stone, Carter remained committed to hiring Gillian Anderson and was at last reluctantly granted approval by the network. Carter recalls, "I sort of staked my pilot and my career at the time on Gillian. I feel vindicated every day now" (Wild, 1996, Chris Carter section, para. 26).

Gillian Anderson was a teenager in the early 1980s when she began acting in community theater in Grand Rapids, Michigan. Following high school, she pursued her interest in the field by attending the Goodman Theater School of Drama at DePaul University in Chicago, where she earned a Bachelor's degree in Fine Arts in 1990. She then moved to New York City and occasionally performed in off-Broadway plays while working as a waitress before relocating to Los Angeles two years later. Less than one week after being cast in the role of Scully in early 1993, the 24-year-old headed north to Vancouver, British Columbia, to film the pilot episode of *The X-Files*.

Despite her controversial casting, Gillian Anderson went on to win an Emmy Award, a Golden Globe Award, and two Screen Actor's Guild Awards for her lead role as Special Agent Dana Scully on *The X-Files*. She also won peer and critical accolades for performances in several films made during the few times she was able to break away from her demanding taping schedule, including *The Mighty* (1998), *Playing By Heart* (1999) and, most notably, the tragic lead character in *The House of Mirth* (2000).

The X-Files changed Gillian Anderson's life in many ways, not the least of which entailed a growing concern for social causes coupled with her emerging ability as a celebrity to bring attention to those causes. Her initial involvement in charity organizations stemmed from her family's personal experience with the genetic disorder, neurofibromatosis. Gillian Anderson has since used her celebrity capital to raise awareness as well as funds for non-profit support groups that assist families living with the disorder. As her fame grew, so also did her association with various other organizations, such as the Feminist Majority Foundation, Buskaid (a charitable trust benefiting young musicians in South Africa), and the Trevor Project (which assists gay and questioning youth). Gillian Anderson's dedicated efforts to advocate social causes, in addition to her inextricable identification with Scully, have garnered her enduring recognition and respect as a celebrity role model.

CHAPTER III

REVIEW OF LITERATURE

Analyzing a popular culture construct that encompasses elements of text, press discourse, star perspective, and audience activity necessarily calls for an inclusive theoretical framework. Surveying the historical development of a study's grounding theory as well as providing a working knowledge of the specific cultural milieu in which a discourse circulates is essential. Equally significant is the manner in which these various components are integrated into a cohesive whole. The following review of literature attempts to achieve these objectives by rendering a meaningful synthesis of several areas relevant to a critique on the cultural construct of celebrity role models. The two broad categories on which this analysis is structured are feminist media theory and fan-star theory. Within these subject areas, principles of stereotypes and spectatorship, negotiation, fan-star relationships, identification, and stardom are all considered in the examination of celebrity role models. The chapter closes with a review of scholarship on *The X-Files* and a summary of the research questions guiding the issues explored in this project.

Feminist Media Theory

At its root, "all forms of feminist theory share the basic idea that gender is a socially constructed phenomenon, a set of learned behaviors and attitudes, rather than some natural and therefore immutable condition" (Mumford, 1998, p. 116). Regarding its practical usage, feminist theater scholar Gayle Austin (1990) simply states, "a feminist approach to anything means paying attention to women" (p. 1). In addition to these significations, central to feminism is the impetus for political and social change that produces tangible improvements in the lives of women. Examining how this can be accomplished, providing resources to effect such change, and highlighting those progressive moments and movements that oftentimes go unobserved are all facilitated through feminist theory.

This examination is built on the foundation of feminist theory. Though feminism is appropriated in myriad ways, depending on the goals of those who invoke its tenets, I employ it here to illuminate how a female television character, the female actor who portrays her, and a subculture of female fans that admire them both, cooperatively negotiate particular interests and needs within the celebrity role model construct. Specific to television, feminist theory helps to uncover the pervasiveness of gender role stereotyping inherent to the medium, while simultaneously revealing multiple spaces of feminist influence found internal and external to popular representations of women.

Images of Women

Early work in feminist media studies primarily concentrated on how women were represented through character treatment, as supported by mechanisms of dialogue and narrative. Although television and film promoted both positive and negative images of women, feminists necessarily focused on the profusion of negative portrayals, thereby demonstrating the dearth of positive media representations. Many feminist critics in the 1970s perceived the media as powerful cultural reinforcers of patriarchal values that elevated the social position of men and marginalized the contributions of women, chiefly through stereotypic depictions. An example of sex-role stereotyping on television is that of women characters sequestered to the private realm of the home, contentedly functioning as supportive wives and mothers, while their husbands or other male authority figures enjoy the privilege of the public sphere, freely operating in dominant roles. Second wave feminists who interpreted the effects of popular culture to be dangerously influential and far-reaching felt "a deep conviction that women's oppression was very much related to mass media representations and that change was not only urgent, but possible" (Brunsdon, D'Acci, and Spigel, 1997, p. 5). Researchers relied heavily on content analysis methodology to delineate the specific ways and the degree to which women were portrayed and correspondingly oppressed. By thus drawing attention to the extreme inequity in images of women, feminist media critics hoped to bring about social and political change that would result in more fair representations of imaginary women and, hopefully, more regard for real women. As Suzanna Danuta

Walters (1998) describes, the "images of women approach...was largely *descriptive* of the offending representations and then, *prescriptively*, argued for more inclusion and more diversity" (p. 224).

A momentous early critique on how women are represented in popular culture is Betty Friedan's *The Feminine Mystique* (1963). Using images found in women's magazines and advertising, Friedan outlines the post-war construction of America's celebrated ideal of womanhood – what she calls the "happy housewife heroine." Friedan argues that such representations of women are false images, or stereotypes, that ultimately work to limit *real* women's individual and collective aspirations. Ten years later, Marjorie Rosen composed *Popcorn Venus* (1973), a volume analyzing women's roles in cinema since 1900. Comparable to Friedan's examination of trends in images of women found in popular print material, Rosen tracks representations of women within the cinematic context. As social roles of real women shifted and expanded throughout the twentieth century in concert with economic realities, so did filmic depictions, though not resulting in an accurate reflection of society's forward changes. Those with a stake in maintaining men's dominance over women instead responded by invoking popular cinema to culturally contain advancements made in women's social condition. Often discussed in tandem with Rosen's study is Molly Haskell's *From Reverence to Rape* (1974), which also takes issue with cinema's historic treatment of women. Patricia Erens (1990) encapsulates these parallel image studies: "Both works chronicled the changing image of women in Hollywood films and both used sociological approaches which highlighted how the female characters related to the history of the era, how these characters were stereotyped, how active or passive they were, how much screen time they were allotted, and whether they served as positive or negative models for women in the audience" (p. xvi).

In terms of television, the collection *Hearth and Home* (Tuchman, Daniels, and Benet, 1978) likewise employs effects studies and content analysis techniques to expose the prevalence of sex-role stereotyping broadcast to living rooms across the country and around the world up through the mid-1970s. Subscribing to the theoretical model that media reflect society's dominant (i.e., patriarchal) values while simultaneously working to socialize audience members into stereotypical gender roles, Tuchman (1978) is duly concerned with what it means for girls growing up amidst unfavorable televisual depictions of women: "Girls exposed to 'television women' may hope to be homemakers when they are adults, but not workers outside the home. Indeed, as adults these girls may resist work outside the home unless necessary for the economic well being of their families" (p. 7). Tuchman's final conclusion that television fare illustrates the "symbolic annihilation of women" is discouraging, leaving little room for girls to either think beyond what they see on television as they go through the crucial process of identity formation and socialization or to recognize and exploit spaces of feminist resistance that exist within those television texts. Nevertheless, Tuchman's work is considered exemplary not only in demonstrating that conventional gender roles are reproduced and reinforced by the culture industry, but that televisual representations of women can be even more disparaged than their real life counterparts.

Woman as Image

In due course, alternatives to the abundant studies on "images of women" began to emerge, mainly from feminist film theorists who advocated what they deemed a more sophisticated approach of textual analysis predicated on semiology and Lacanian-inflected psychoanalysis. Foremost of these scholars is Laura Mulvey, whose 1975 renowned piece "Visual pleasure and narrative cinema" continues to influence feminist media studies. Mulvey investigates cinematic spectatorship; specifically, how the film text and the cinematic environment construct gendered subjects. Mulvey's argument is structured through narrative and visual analysis of the filmic discourse and the presumed spectators' relationship with that discourse. She concludes that no authentic viewing position exists for women within the male-dominated film apparatus.

One of several issues raised by Mulvey is that of the active/male and passive/female dichotomy. When applied to film, this split is represented by a female character serving as passive "image" to the male character, who is the active "bearer of the look." She explains, "The determining male gaze projects its fantasy onto the female figure which is styled accordingly. In their traditional exhibitionist role women are simultaneously looked at and displayed, with their appearance coded for strong visual and erotic impact so that they can be said to connote *to-be-looked-*

at-ness" (p. 11). In addition to actively looking at and hence controlling the eroticized female object, the male protagonist is correspondingly responsible for driving the narrative forward. By this mechanism he directs the look of the spectator, who, seeing through his eyes, identifies with his (male) position. Mulvey theorizes the controlling look of the leading male character is one of three masculine "gazes" that constitutes cinematic texts. The other two gazes entail the look of the camera, manipulated through framing as determined by male directors and cinematographers, and the look of male spectators, who are the presumed subjects of narrative cinema. All three gazes combine to produce a patriarchal filmic discourse wherein the gendered processes of camera and spectator gazes are concealed through the privileged gaze of the male hero. Mulvey argues that this masculine composition of cinematic visual pleasure excludes any express space for authentic female identification.

Reformulating what Gledhill (1988) calls Mulvey's "cine-psychoanalytic" theoretical model (p. 66), Mary Ann Doane (1982) analyzes a genre that is specifically targeted to female audiences – the "woman's film" of 1940s Hollywood. Starting with the knowledge that these films were produced for and largely seen by women, Doane examines how female spectators are constructed within a masculine filmic discourse that, by Mulvey's account, cannot accommodate a feminine spectator-position. Her analysis demonstrates a profusion of oppressive themes featuring loss and punishment endured by tragic female heroines of the woman's film. Doane concludes that, even when presented with starring images of women with whom they are meant to identify, female spectators are still denied a genuine feminine spectator-position within the masculine-structured cinematic context. As summarized by Liesbet van Zoonen (1994), "the female spectator can only be construed as becoming narcissistically immersed in the cinematic (female) object, or as suffering 'masculinization' by identifying with the (male) hero" (p. 91). Though she arrives at her conclusions through somewhat different means than Mulvey, Doane's prospects for both female protagonists and female moviegoers are similarly pessimistic, if not direr.

A "Cultural Turn"

The contrasting perspectives of prevailing feminist media inquiry of the 1970s – sociologically-based "images of women" and psychoanalytically-inspired "woman as image" – were soon challenged by critics who charged that neither approach adequately accounts for the complexities of media production and reception. While both models examine concepts of "image," both also heavily rely on textual analysis (via either content analysis or semiotic interpretation), which neglects important contextual elements such as how culture industry producers shape representations and how media consumers interpret those representations. One such response to studies on sex-role stereotyping is that by Griselda Pollock (1977), who in "What's wrong with images of women?" contests the assumption that media output is a direct reflection of reality, accurate or otherwise. Instead, she argues that representations are formed through a culturally selective process of meaning making, and that it is these fluid processes that should form the basis of media analysis. In regard to Mulvey's "woman as image" formulation, B. Ruby Rich's "In the name of feminist film criticism" (1978/1990) points out that female spectators are active participants within the filmic discourse who oftentimes perceive and resist onscreen patriarchal renderings. Also concerned with restrictive psychoanalytic treatments of cinematic identification is Jackie Stacey (1994), who contends that "the relationship between the unconscious workings of film texts and the identities of actual female spectators in the cinema remains of little or no significance" (p. 135) in most image studies.

Dissatisfaction with, and challenges to, early forms of feminist media studies are illustrative of what Michèle Barrett (1992) characterizes as a "cultural turn" within feminist theory. Jackson and Jones (1998) sum up this transition from an emphasis on overarching social structures to issues of individual subjectivity: "Where once feminist academic production was preoccupied with such issues as the economic and sexual exploitation of women, attention has shifted to the pleasures of popular cultural consumption and the fashioning of cultural identities" (p. 6-7). As an approach that Sue Thornham (1997) credits with accounting for "the *whole* of the communicative process" (p. xv), cultural studies emphasizes the agency of individuals to be active cultural participants and makers of meaning. It is characterized by an interdisciplinary research methodology that integrates textual and ethnographic critique in an effort to discern individual and social experiences within a historical-cultural context. By considering the implications of both texts and social practices of popular culture, cultural studies provides a way to move beyond the confines of the "woman as image" focus on ideological power over assumed spectators, and into the lived experiences of actual people. Compared to "images of women" perspectives, cultural studies facilitates a more intricate understanding of "reality" than what is permitted under simplistic reflectionist models.

Specific methodological contributions to the field of feminist critique owed to cultural studies include reception theory, spectatorship studies, and ethnographic investigations (Walters, 1998, p. 228). These are all analytic frameworks that privilege media consumers as active agents in the cultural construction of meaning. John Corner (1999) calls the burgeoning of reception studies (a fundamental principle of cultural studies), "the most significant new focus in the television research of the 1980s" (p. 80). What this focus on audiences and reception processes prompted in more than just feminist circles was a sincere interest in how real women experience, interpret, and are affected by media fare.

The eminent "Encoding/Decoding" essay by Stuart Hall (1980) has been paramount to the infusion of cultural theory into feminist media studies as well as numerous other research disciplines. Hall's encoding/decoding model of communication posits that media product is encoded from an ideologically dominant frame of reference and is therefore imbued with meanings that preserve the hegemonic order. Though, while encoded messages may relay determinate points of view, the process of audience decoding affords a site of "struggle" over those denotations. According to Hall, decoding, which occurs at the moment of reception, can be classified into three types of interpretive strategies – dominant, oppositional, and negotiated. Media consumers employing a dominant reading strategy essentially agree with and accept the intended ideological meanings of texts. Oppositional readers clearly recognize but deliberately reject the dominant values encoded in a text, substituting alternative interpretations for those intended by media producers. Receivers who negotiate media messages are amenable to the overall dominant meanings of texts while at the same time resistant to certain aspects that do not apply to or reflect their own social circumstances. It is during the process of negotiation that people actively work to manipulate and re-appropriate the textual message so that it more closely conforms to their individual needs.

Distinct from his rendering of "negotiation" as a reading *type*, Hall also uses the term to account for a *process* of meaning production. This process is unique to the three distinct moments in the communication system of production encoding, textual manifestation, and reception decoding, wherein meaning is internally negotiated. For example, the text itself operates as a site of negotiation insofar as it affords opportunity for actors, through performance, to alter cultural meanings apart from producers' intent. Receivers later negotiate this same text as they inscribe it with meaning significant to their own lives.

Negotiation

Christine Gledhill (1988) draws on Hall's encoding/decoding explanatory model in her feminist analysis of meaning production, "Pleasurable Negotiations." In accordance with the tenets of cultural studies, Gledhill maintains, "we require a theory of texts which can also accommodate the historical existence of social audiences" (p. 67), for which she likewise proposes the term "negotiation." Gledhill contends that ideological meaning, especially as it relates to definitions of women, is not fixed, but rather continually (re)negotiated within and at intersections of production, text, and reception processes. Such an understanding of meaning-making necessitates examination at *all* levels if proper recovery is to be made about where and how female subjectivity is relationally constructed. Asserting that textual meaning "is neither imposed, nor passively imbibed, but arises out of a struggle or negotiation between competing frames of reference, motivation and experience" (p. 68), Gledhill's framework is an attempt to balance the hegemonic authority of textually constructed meanings with the lived socio-historical experiences of real women audience members. In context of feminist media criticism, she creates a theoretical space between deterministic "woman as image" analyses and the "images of women" emphasis on effects in an effort to more thoroughly account for the fluidity of cultural production. Recognizing that "textual analysis cannot alone determine the progressiveness or otherwise of a particular work," Gledhill charges the feminist critic with analyzing "the conditions and possibilities of reading" (p. 74).

Ethnographic investigations into the agency of female media consumers, as well as analysis of production elements that form media product, are thus equally important components to critical interpretation of popular culture.

A notable example of Gledhill's analytical concept of cultural negotiation is found in Julie D'Acci's (1994) commendable work on how femininity and feminism are (re)defined within various circulating discourses surrounding the early 1980s television series, *Cagney & Lacey*. D'Acci examines all three primary components of the television apparatus – production, text, and reception – toward building a comprehensive case study of the controversial program. Aiming to uncover the intricacies of popular culture constructions of femininity within a specific socio-historical setting, D'Acci's analysis reveals the variable nature of cultural production: "[M]eanings are in constant tension, in which network television, its programs (or texts), its viewers, and its historical contexts are sites for the negotiation of numerous definitions and discourses, with certain ones achieving more power or 'discursive authority' at specific moments and for specific participants than others" (p. 3). Relative to other feminist media studies that focus on textual analysis and/or audience interpretations, D'Acci pays considerable attention to production activities. Vital to comprehending the encoding process, the production arena is oftentimes difficult to probe in light of the entertainment industry's reluctance to allow outsiders research privileges, and is therefore a neglected element in most critiques.

Also adopting negotiation as an organizing principle for her own ethnographic study is Jackie Stacey in *Star Gazing* (1994), who examines and elaborates on operations of fan-star identification. Arguing the need for "an interactive model of text/audience/context to account for the complexity of the viewing process" (p. 47) within the cinematic setting, Stacey accordingly combines psychoanalytic principles of feminist film theory with ethnographic inquiry in her reevaluation of the female film spectator. Stacey's usage of the concept of negotiation extends further yet to the relationship between fans and stars, which involves the "complex negotiation of self and other, image and ideal, and subject and object. Screen image and self-image are connected through a dialectical interplay…" (p. 227). Stacey suggests, along the lines of Gledhill, that negotiation processes are not confined internally to areas of production, text, and reception, but also occur interdependently among these three distinct domains. For example, fans that expropriate characteristics of their favored stars to transform their own identities – what Stacey refers to as "extra-cinematic identificatory practices" – are engaging in a process of cultural negotiation between themselves (reception) and the star image (production).

Fan-Star Theory

Accessibility to the famous – or, at least to information about the famous – has never been greater in light of the abundance of star texts available for general consumption. Cultural critic Neal Gabler (1998) notes, "By the 1980s virtually every general-interest magazine in America – and in the rest of the world for that matter – featured a celebrity on its cover and one celebrity story after another inside" (p. 148). Fans, especially, who are attracted to certain imaginary television characters have ample opportunity to acquire a plethora of information on the performers behind the portrayals.

Examining the relational dynamics of fans and stars is a crucial step in understanding the cultural construct of a celebrity role model. A star is a role model insofar as appreciative fans have deemed her such. Surveying various definitions and theories on the nature of how fans relate to stars and how stars themselves operate within the realm of stardom enables a more informed analysis of the celebrity role model text. The following subsections establish the idea that media fans are generally ordinary people who, in the course of everyday negotiation of their social surroundings, develop imaginary relationships with favored stars. The structure of these relationships is addressed with the caveat that the referenced theories on audience-star relationships are based on film stars and the cinematic experience. Similar to other scholarship noted in this review of literature, these concepts are applied to the medium of television and its stars. Furthermore, the terms "star" and "celebrity" are not differentiated conceptually, and are therefore used here interchangeably.

Defining Fans

Joli Jensen (1992) offers a critique of the elitism with which academics and journalists tend to regard fans, contending that, "The literature on fandom is haunted by images of deviance. The fan is consistently characterized (referencing the term's origins) as a potential fanatic. This means that fandom is seen as excessive, bordering on deranged, behavior" (p. 9). Concerning media fans, she continues: "The fan is understood to be, at least implicitly, a result of celebrity – the fan is defined as a *response* to the star system. This means that passivity is ascribed to the fan – he or she is seen as being brought into (enthralled) existence by the modern celebrity system, via the mass media" (p. 10). Jensen argues that the bias on the part of social scientists to view fans as lacking and vulnerable has worked to obscure any true understanding of how regular people manage their lives in today's media-saturated environment (p. 25-26), and that there is need for more scholarly literature that "explores fandom as a normal, everyday cultural or social phenomenon" (p. 13).

In the same vein that Jensen sees fan activity as commonplace among ordinary people, Abercrombie and Longhurst (1998) define fans as "those people who become particularly attached to certain programmes or stars within the context of relatively heavy mass media use. They are individuals who are not yet in contact with other people who share their attachments..." (p. 138). A person who sets time aside on a regular basis to watch a favored television series would fall under this definition of fan. Abercrombie and Longhurst further develop their topography of fan behavior by invoking the term "cultist" to account for fans that proceed beyond their immediate social environment in pursuit of fan activities and more focused media usage. This practice of media specialization results in the formation of "very explicit attachments to stars or to particular programmes" (p. 139) that, in turn, leads to participation in a community founded on shared media interests. While provocative, their designation of certain fan activity as "cultist" in nature may make the task of legitimatizing fandom as a normal and acceptable cultural practice more difficult. Lastly, "enthusiast" is used to describe yet a rarer type of fan – those who engage in "producerly" activities. According to Abercrombie and Longhurst, fan subgroups of *Star Trek* are fitting examples of enthusiasts (p. 139).

Writing about *Star Trek* fandom, Henry Jenkins (1992) concurs with Jensen's (1992) assessment of widely held misrepresentations of fans: "Building on the word's traditional links to madness and demonic possession, news reports frequently characterize fans as psychopaths whose frustrated fantasies of intimate relationships with stars or unsatisfied desires to achieve their own stardom take violent and antisocial forms" (p. 13). In fact, Jenkins' primary objective for analyzing the intricacies of fan behavior is to counter such pejorative connotations of the term. It is notable, then, that he undertakes a study of an oft-ridiculed group in his attempt to legitimize fans, especially considering his interpretation that the *Star Trek* community's manifestation of fandom is "in no sense representative of the audience at large" (p. 286). Because Jenkins' description of fans as being productive members of alternative social communities (e.g., fan clubs) is rather narrow, his discussion is somewhat inadequate for exploring various other fan activities practiced by the "audience at large." While his treatment of *Star Trek* fandom is highly commendable, limiting the definition of what fans do to very specific community involvement is restrictive and consequently neglectful of the many layers of fan experience. The major contribution of Jenkins' comprehensive analysis, bolstered by his own personal involvement in the community he explores, is the conclusion that "fans cannot as a group be dismissed as intellectually inferior; they often are highly educated, articulate people who come from the middle classes..." (p. 18).

While there are doubtless numerous other definitions and uses of the term "fan," this overview demonstrates that writers must deliberately frame the word, or its equivalent, to fit what they hope to accomplish through their argument. The meanings of "fan" and "fandom" are far from fixed.

Fan-Star Relationships

Horton and Wohl (1956) present an early critique of fan-star relationships, labeling the illusory face-to-face relationships fans form with celebrities as "para-social interactions." Seeking to intimately know and be known by the famous, fans develop a unilateral connection with celebrities that simulates actual social relations. Such para-social interactions are considered generally benign until fans, stereotypically the socially inept and psychologically fragile, according to the authors attempt to subrogate their imagined friendships with stars for genuine relationships. It is at this point, "when the para-social relationship becomes a substitute for autonomous social participation, when it proceeds in absolute defiance of objective reality, that it can be regarded as pathological" (p. 223). Being unable to effectively engage in authentic relationships, along with nurturing a fantasy of shared intimacy with celebrities, marks these fans as aberrant partakers of popular culture.

Building on Horton and Wohl's formulation of fan-star para-social interactions is Richard Schickel (1985) in his discussion of an "illusion of intimacy" (p. 4) that fans construct around their favored celebrities. Schickel contends that the socially acceptable courteous manner in which strangers treat one another upon meeting is completely disregarded when fans presume inappropriate intimate relationships with celebrities: "Most of us retain...a sense of otherness, a decent wariness that protects both ourselves and the stranger from intrusion. But that shyness...is not operative when we are dealing with celebrities. Thanks to television and the rest of the media we *know* them, or think we do. ... [W]e have internalized them, unconsciously made them a apart of our consciousness, just as if they were, in fact, friends" (p. 4). Schickel sees such fantasies of celebrity friendship as fans' attempt to attain vicarious celebrity status themselves. This condition is produced by an individual's failure to establish her own reality-based individual identity and earn acknowledgment within her existing social sphere.

Working from the same assumption that fan attachments to celebrities are para-social and illusory in nature, John Caughey (1984) labels these connections "imaginary social relationships" (p. 241). He concurs that "people characterize unmet media figures as if they were intimately involved with them" (p. 33), but, significantly, departs from the notion that fannish behavior is somehow deviant. He asserts that such pseudo-social relationships are healthy and even necessary in contemporary culture. Through identification with particular media figures, fans are afforded the opportunity to fulfill certain goals and aspirations they might not have otherwise. In short, celebrities function as ideal role models whom fans strive to emulate. This imitative role modeling can reverberate throughout a person's authentic interactions, positively affecting their material relationships with family, friends, and co-workers. For example, imitating a star's aura of confidence as she speaks to the press may inspire a fan to exude similar confidence when making a presentation before peers. According to Caughey, "Such relatively superficial influences are often part of a deeper identification in which the media figure's values and plans are incorporated into the fan's social behavior. ... Operating in his or her own identity as someone who wants to act like the ideal figure, the individual may employ the media figure as a mentor or guide" (p. 59). Fans establish for themselves celebrity role models to which they can turn for direction, motivation, support, and comfort as they go about their daily routine. Furthermore, celebrity role models potentially have lasting influence over a fan's lifetime, long after initial admiration for a star fades (p. 69). The desirable characteristics a fan adopts through imitative behavior may evolve into an integral facet of her own identity – what she learns from the celebrity eventually being incorporated into her own persona, often quite naturally.

Whereas Horton and Wohl (1956) and Schickel (1985) provide useful insights into the phenomenon of celebrity-focused illusory relationships, they do nothing to recover the positive elements of such fantasies for those who engage them. Caughey's conceptualization of fan-star imaginary relationships not only counters the common misunderstanding that fan behavior is suspect, but he goes on to embrace it as completely normal and essential to the psychological health of individuals and culture at large. He interprets fan relationships with stars primarily as social relationships rather than mere "esthetic appreciation" (p. 40), suggesting a more equal balance of power between fan and star. Instead of the fan embarrassing either herself or the admired star through illusory interactions, she develops creative thinking and social skills that will enrich her unique contributions to society.

Identification

Leo Handel (1950), who performed early research on film audiences, distinguishes several overlapping types of star-audience identification. Most relevant to this study is the type of identification known as "idealisation and idolization." Primarily comprised of young and female fans, Handel describes it as a bond established with a star that extends into a fan's personal life and which thus affects behavior. Andrew Tudor (1974) adapts Handel's work on audiences in his formulation of various levels of relationships audience members may experience with regard to stars. Differentiating between connections that take place during the movie-going experience ("context specific") and those that transpire outside of the cinematic environment ("diffuse"), Tudor's categorization encompasses four types of relationships. "Emotional affinity" occurs when "the audience feels a loose attachment to a particular protagonist" during the course of watching a film; this level of involvement is generally tenuous and considered "standard" among moviegoers. Tudor designates the second, higher range of involvement as "self-identification," which entails an audience member positioning herself "in the same situation and persona of the star," though still within the confines of the narrative. Progressing to diffuse activities, the relationship type called "imitation" involves "the star acting as some sort of model for the audience;" prevalent among adolescents, examples include copying stars' clothing and hairstyles. Lastly, "projection" is used to describe "the point at which the [imitation] process becomes more than a simple mimicking" (p. 80-82). Projection is a condition whereby fans take into account how stars would behave in certain situations, and then attempt to imitate that supposed behavior in their own lives. Tudor locates both imitation and projection as practices that are most common among the young, seeing them as losing "force" once people transition into adulthood. His classification of these diffuse connections (which transpire *outside* of the cinematic environment) as basically youth-inspired processes implies that only context specific identification with stars (that which occurs *during* film watching) is the normal adult response.

It is the extra-cinematic activities that fans engage in – what Tudor calls imitation and projection – that Jackie Stacey (1994) principally elaborates on in *Star Gazing*. Her study demonstrates that these processes are not reserved only for young people, as Tudor would suggest, but that elements of star imitation and projection can extend well into and possibly throughout an adult's life. Stacey is predominantly interested in how gender intersects with the range of fan-star identification and, accordingly, conducts an ethnographic investigation into women's reminiscences of the 1940s and 1950s female movie stars they adored. She develops a multi-layered model to illustrate three main themes of female audience response to cinema: escapism, identification, and consumerism, with considerable emphasis on the second of these categories – identification. Similar to Tudor's framework, Stacey divides identification into two types of processes termed "cinematic identificatory fantasies," which occur at the time of film viewing, and "extra-cinematic identificatory practices," which take place beyond the cinematic context. Connections audience members form with stars during the course of a movie are deemed fantasies because they only exist within the spectator's imagination, usually involving feelings of "devotion," "adoration," and "worship" toward the idolized star as she appears on the screen. Stacey explains that these experiences "make little reference to the relationship between self-image and Hollywood ideal and focus instead upon the wonder the spectator remembers feeling in relation to the star" (p. 143). Forms of identification that draw spectators into a more relational affinity with certain stars are classified in terms of "transcendence," described by Stacey as a unidirectional "temporary loss of self and the adoption of a star persona" (p. 151), and of "aspiration/inspiration," involving varying degrees of identity transformation practiced by spectators in response to star images. It is at this point of aspiration/inspiration where spectator fantasies evolve into fan cultural activity, thus forming the basis for what Stacey calls extra-cinematic identificatory practices, itself comprised of four subtypes: "pretending," "resembling," "imitating," and "copying."

While each of these extra-cinematic practices involves a spectator's active pursuit of identity transformation via mimic of a star's persona, only "imitation" presupposes material changes in that fan's "behaviour and activities" (p. 167). Stacey describes this subtype as "actual imitation of a star or of her particular characteristics in a particular film" (p. 161). Implicated in Stacey's schema is the idea that spectators who engage in imitative practices do so selectively; that is, such identificatory conduct entails only a "partial taking on of some aspect of a star's identity" (p. 163). Adoption of only specific characteristics possessed by favored stars suggests that this type of active fan is discriminating and practical in her desire to modify her identity. She is a rational subject who intentionally chooses the facets of a star's persona that would be beneficial were she to incorporate them into her own identity. Unfortunately, Stacey does not pursue this avenue since she does not elaborate on the spectator processes of extra-cinematic imitation. Her work, however, does provide a solid structural framework in addition to a stepping off point for further research in the area of fan-star identification and activity. Imitation need not be limited to singular self-improvement such as when a fan builds confidence by emulating a star's assertive nature. Imitative behavior can move beyond the personal to include a fan's participation in the preferred social and political activities of the admired star, as well.

Stardom

Because media fans exist in relation to stars and vice versa, a consideration of fandom is not complete without a discussion of stardom. In his distinguished volume, *Stars*, Richard Dyer (1979) delves the ideological significance of stardom with a close examination of the constructed star image. His treatment assumes that "stars have a privileged position in the definition of social roles and types, and this must have real consequences in terms of how people believe they can and should behave" (p. 8). Defining star image as a group of media texts comprising "promotion, publicity, films, and criticism and commentaries" (p. 60), he establishes early on that "we are dealing with the stars in terms of their signification, not with them as real people. The fact that they are also real people is an important aspect of how they signify, but we never know them directly as real people, only as they are to be found in media texts" (p. 2). Throughout his analysis, Dyer discusses stardom in terms of acting processes, characterization, and projected star image, but never in terms of any genuine personal or political activities of stars-as-people. The emergence of an authentic person behind the star image is limited under his theoretical formulation.

In his second book, *Heavenly Bodies*, Dyer (1986) further seeks to discover "the social significance of stars" by revisiting the issue of how audience members experience them. This time from the perspective of the audience, Dyer explores the public/private dichotomy of stars' lives and the obsessive desire of audience subcultures to *really know* celebrities beyond their image: "Whether caught in the unmediated moment of the close-up, uncovered by the biographer's display of ruthless uncovering, or present in the star's indubitable sincerity and authenticity, we have a privileged reality to hang on to, the reality of the star's private self" (p. 11). People are interested in celebrities because of their ability to "speak to us in terms we can understand about things that are important to us" (p. 16). Stars publicly personify the struggles, contradictions, and resolutions that people experience in our own everyday lives, which makes the aspiration to know them, and thus ourselves, all the more powerful.

In the introduction to his anthology titled *Star Texts*, Jeremy Butler (1991) draws on Dyer (1979) to define star image as a "polysemic construct" made up of various media texts that revolve around a celebrity, including performance narratives, televised and published interviews, promotional campaigns, and press coverage (p. 12). Like Dyer, Butler argues that, if the concepts of stardom and celebrity are to be rightly understood, then all aspects of star image should be investigated. Refreshingly, Butler deliberately highlights the importance of television in his critique, a medium noted by Dyer only insofar as to acknowledge his extensive analysis is "broadly applicable to these other kinds of star" (Dyer, 1979, p. 3). Compared to film studies that primarily rely on textual analysis for ideological critique, Butler claims that, "The empirical, social-scientific approach of most television research has led to a nearly total neglect of the significance of performance and star image in television. ... There has been a similar paucity of analyses from nonempirical, critical studies of television as well" (Butler, 1991, p. 14). He maintains that television stars-as-actors and stars-as-people are vital components of the public's captivation with media texts and therefore warrant more scholarly attention (p. 15).

Looking beyond the scope of film and television star studies to the broader arena of celebrity studies is P. David Marshall in *Celebrity and Power* (1997). His work diverts from Dyer's and Butler's focus on image by conceptualizing stars/celebrities as examples of ultimate individuality, declaring the celebrity to be "the independent individual par excellence" who "represents the meaning of freedom and accessibility in a culture" (p. 246). Expounding on the functional role and practical significance of the celebrity system, Marshall theorizes that people admire and identify with celebrities toward the promise of likewise transforming themselves into autonomous social agents. Through both real and fictional incarnations of a celebrity, "the audience can construct the 'perfect hero,' where the star's actions serve as exemplary models for a particular community" (p. 187). Marshall contends that the degree of a celebrity's influence is commensurate to the authority granted her by audience members. More authority, and thereby more power, is accorded to stars whose "messages" align with individuals' own goals and aspirations. Stars that depict sympathetic lead characters are more likely to convey positive messages that form the basis for identification.

Scholarship on *The X-Files*

From its inception as a televisual text, *The X-Files* has been considered through a variety of scholarly lenses, most of which offer ideological analysis. An early collection of critical research specific to the program is contained in the 1996 volume *Deny All Knowledge: Reading the X-Files* (Lavery, Hague, and Cartwright), which features discussions on how issues of gender, language, fan activity, and culture are negotiated within the discursive parameters of the *X-Files*. Other academic treatments have explored the series in relation to paranoia and cynicism (Markley, 1997); the authority of science, government, and gender (Bellon, 1999); private and public domains of home and work (Bertsch, 1998); postmodernism (Kellner, 1999); and epistemological consequences of faith versus science (Westerfelhaus and Combs, 1998). However, one significant perspective relatively scarce in the canon of *X-Files* scholarship is textual representation and viewer reception of female protagonist Agent Scully. Wilcox and Williams (1996) do provide an examination of how partners Mulder and Scully successfully function as gender-reversed binary opposites, one exhibiting traits coded as feminine (Mulder) and one as masculine (Scully), while Lisa Parks (1996) presents a theoretical analysis along the lines of Donna Haraway on the monstrous body of Scully. However, aside from being based on less than one-third of *The X-Files* episode repertoire, these arguments are exclusively textual in nature and thus limited to ideological interpretation.

More recently published accounts have partially filled the void in terms of exploring feminist aspects of *The X-Files* in general, and Scully and Gillian Anderson in particular. In *Tough Girls* (1999), Sherrie Inness discusses the containment of female toughness with respect to Scully as character and Anderson as actor. However, her tendency to rigidly typify Scully as tough or soft, masculine or feminine, right or wrong, fails to allow for an adequate assessment of the nuanced character or for insight into how viewers might meaningfully negotiate her. Such a cursory understanding of *The X-Files* (which rarely, if ever, operates within concrete boundaries) does not lend itself to a well-formed ideological analysis of its female protagonist. Nevertheless, despite such broad generalizations of both Scully and

Anderson, Inness' contribution is still useful for its focus on the two principal female images of *The X-Files*.

In a more comprehensive review , Linda Badley (2000) thoughtfully draws on her extensive knowledge of *The X-Files* text in an exploration of Scully and Gillian Anderson as postmodern, postfeminist, and posthumanist cultural icons. She frames her innovative case by stating these two female celebrities must be considered together, given their corresponding positions as popular feminist role models. Following a discussion supplemented with multiple examples drawn from *X-Files* episodes, Badley reluctantly concludes that Scully's role, though pioneering for television women, ultimately sustains the patriarchal status quo. Her evaluation that Gillian Anderson mirrors Scully's postfeminist agenda is far less supported, though, and indicative of the intellectual need to focus more attention on stars themselves. About Scully and Anderson, Badley claims, "With few exceptions, the two are consistent: they/she stand for individual effort and reward in a context of career as opposed to working for social change, and for setting a high-profile example in a world of men rather than discovering her commonality with other women" (p. 87). An accurate interpretation of how someone works toward affecting social change and shares in the company of other women can really only be determined through a close reading of the subject herself, which Badley does not perform.

Another scholar who is actively engaged in the text under study is Sarah Wakefield (2001), who focuses on an online community to which she belongs called the "Order of the Blessed Saint Scully the Enigmatic" (OBSSE). The fan group is unique in that it is structured around the heroic character Scully and not her real life counterpart, Gillian Anderson. Wakefield uses OBSSE, a forum initially organized in 1995 for purposes of collectively "worshipping" the *X-Files* female lead, to demonstrate how a specific subgroup of fans have "poached the character of Agent Scully, making her into saint, everywoman, and sexpot" (p. 136). In the process, this participatory community has evolved into a safe space of "sisterhood," where friendships and discussion about more than just *The X-Files* flourish.

Inness (1999), Badley (2000), and Wakefield (2001) are representative of a handful of academics who have moved beyond the limits of *The X-Files* discrete televisual text in their analyses of the show, particularly as it relates to the significance of Scully and Gillian Anderson. Concerning the Agent Mulder character who, as the impetus for investigating X-File cases, is paid considerably more critical attention than his female partner, David Duchovny as actor is likewise academically neglected to the same degree as is Gillian Anderson. The fact that numerous scholars have devoted time and energy to critique *The X-Files* corroborates its status as a popular culture icon worthy of critical attention. The fact that only few of the analyses examine audience or production (e.g., star) aspects of this long-running series reveals these areas are in need of further exploration. The following analysis attempts to address that deficiency.

Research Questions

Examined in this study is the cultural construct of a contemporary female celebrity role model. Specifically taken up are the elements comprising that construct, the interrelation of those elements, and the potential social significance of celebrity role models. *The X-Files'* character Scully, actor Gillian Anderson, popular press discourse, and a subgroup of online female fans, are used to illustrate and interpret this phenomenon. The approach of analyzing fans and stars in relation to each other aligns with feminist social theorists Jackson and Jones' (1998) exhortation to study "the material actualities of women's everyday experience and examine the ways in which we are represented and represent ourselves within a range of cultural practices" (p. 1). Such exploration, they contend, leads to "cultural understandings of what it means to be a woman" (p. 1). Discovering certain "actualities" of women's lives is accomplished herein through analysis of fan discourse and activity carried out in response to the celebrity images of Scully and Gillian Anderson, while detecting the "ways in which we are represented" is achieved through a textual analysis of the Scully character. An investigation into how Gillian Anderson constructs her own celebrity role model image provides a notable example of how women "represent ourselves."

The three research questions developed to support this feminist examination of the cultural construct of celebrity role models are:

1) How are Scully and Gillian Anderson constructed as role models for women?
2) How does Gillian Anderson negotiate her position of role model?
3) How do women negotiate Scully and Gillian Anderson as role models?

Question 1 is descriptive in nature and intended to form the basis for discussion of Questions 2 and 3. It is comprised of two parts: firstly, it illuminates the construction of Scully as role model via the televisual text; and, secondly, it demonstrates the construction of Gillian Anderson as role model via popular press discourse. To accomplish the first, I draw on general principles from both the "images of women" and "woman as image" perspectives in order to map how the Scully character is representative of real women. While theories on images of women have been discounted in light of more recent sophisticated formulations on the contested image of woman, the basic assumption that role models do exist and potentially exercise influence over viewers should be retained. In my elaboration on Scully as a role model, I take up the implied objective of the images of women approach to locate *positive* female images in the media, though without the encumbrance of content analysis methodology. The more focused textual analysis I perform on *The X-Files* is along the lines of the woman as image theoretical model. Mulvey (1975) is used here to the extent that she provides an explanatory model for the "gaze" of the camera, the principal actors, and the audience. However, the presumption of a standard female viewing position is disregarded in deference to the actual experiences and practices of women fans that are explored under Question 3.

Relevant to the second part of Question 1, my analysis of how Gillian Anderson is constructed as a role model for women is inspired by the cultural studies mandate to examine the socio-historical environment in which specific texts operate. Whereas Scully can simply be explored textually, the image of Gillian Anderson is a synthesis of various popular discourses related to her person. Informed interpretation of how women negotiate Scully and Gillian Anderson (treated in Question 3) can only be obtained through examination of attendant contextual elements. I take as inspiration Gledhill's (1988) concept of cultural negotiation as it pertains to the complexities of meaning production. D'Acci's (1994) work on the television series *Cagney & Lacey* is a prime example of how meaning is (re)negotiated and (re)defined through various discourses, demonstrating the imperativeness of studying the dynamics of circulating cultural discourse.

Question 2 on how Gillian Anderson negotiates her position of role model is fairly unique in scholarship on stars. A historical treatment of what Gillian Anderson has said over the years in regard to her dual status as real and fictional role model is not that unusual. Rather, what distinguishes this from most star studies is that I also examine the subject from within; that is, through a personal interview with the star herself. The analysis of how Gillian Anderson perceives herself and her fans is situated between Dyer's (1979) discussion of the public's desire to *know* the authentic, unmediated self of the star, and the avenue provided by Marshall (1997) for connecting the authority of stars to the identificatory agency of individuals.

Question 3 on how women negotiate Scully and Gillian Anderson as role models is predicated on theories related to fandom and stardom; specifically, the nature of fan-star relationships and fan identification with favored stars. I follow Caughey's (1984) lead in treating such "imaginary social relationships" as natural and even essential to identity formation. I also incorporate his views on fan identification with, and employment of, celebrities as mentors. Finally, vital to my interpretation of fan negotiation processes is Stacey's (1994) theoretical framework on extra-cinematic identificatory practices. I primarily extend her concept of "imitation" in my discussion and analysis of what some women actively *do* in tribute to Scully and Gillian Anderson.

CHAPTER IV

METHODOLOGY

In an effort to produce a thorough analysis that is faithful to its object of study and the points I strive to convey, I chose to examine a televisual text with which I was already familiar – *The X-Files*. I trust that those who have not seen the show will still appreciate the arguments and conclusions set forth in this critique. My hope is that readers will extrapolate the findings of this study on to their own preferred texts, discovering for themselves how cultural artifacts positively affect media consumers. *The X-Files* is merely a tool employed to illustrate the cultural construct of a celebrity role model and, moreover, how media representations and images can influence the activities of engaged fans. To that end, the three research questions guiding this exploration are:

1) How are Scully and Gillian Anderson constructed as role models for women?
2) How does Gillian Anderson negotiate her position of role model?
3) How do women negotiate Scully and Gillian Anderson as role models?

The purpose of Question 1 is to extract specific points within the text of *The X-Files* related to Scully and the context of Gillian Anderson's celebrity image that construct the two women as role models. Question 2 continues the discussion on mediated representations by highlighting the voice of Gillian Anderson – the one person in whom both the imaginary character and the real actor reside. Question 3 rounds out the examination by focusing on the practices of identification and processes of role modeling by fans in response to the images of Scully and Gillian Anderson.

The concept of role model, as it is used here in regard to fans' relationships with real and imaginary media figures, is based on Bandura's (1977) social learning theory. His premise is that people model certain positively reinforced behaviors that they observe in others, thus learning how to internalize those behaviors as part of their own social selves. Role models are not necessarily defined by proximity to the individuals they influence; they can also be accessed via the media, as in the case of characters and stars. It is important to clarify that the function of role models extends beyond merely reinforcing sex-role behavior, which has been the argument traditionally emphasized in liberal feminist media studies utlizing socialization theory. In fact, identifying with role models involves imitating certain aspects of personal conduct and social practices of the admired – behavior that is commonly ascribed to fans.

Textual Analysis of Scully

Heeding Charlotte Brunsdon's (1989) counsel to "retain a notion of the television text" (p. 126) when performing cultural critique, I begin with a textual analysis of *The X-Files* to illustrate how the imaginary character of Scully is constructed as a role model for women. Being the primary conduit for image representation, as well as the site of negotiation between producers and viewers, the text serves a vital role in cultural exchange. Critical attention to textual operations further provides enhanced understanding of both production and reception processes, which are considered here in the person of Gillian Anderson and in the activity of fans.

Each episode of the series was videotaped either from its original broadcast on the FOX television network or by syndicated release on the FX cable network. Since there are 202 episodes in the series' canon, it was clearly not feasible or desirable to deconstruct all of them in order to map the representations of Scully over nine years of broadcast history. Therefore, I chose to closely consider only two of the moderate number of episodes in which her character is pivotal to the story.

The process of selecting particular episodes for textual analysis commenced with a review of the *X-Files* repertoire, beginning with the pilot premiere in September 1993 and ending with the series finale in May 2002. This general examination produced a pool of approximately 30 episodes that are "Scully-centric" in nature; that is, they focus on Scully. To arrive at just two segments to analyze, I overlaid four criteria to this initial pool. The episodes selected for textual analysis must: 1) have aired in different seasons; 2) feature different themes; 3) correspond to a milestone in Gillian Anderson's professional career; and 4) contain familiar points of identification relevant to women's cultural experiences (i.e., not be so paranormal that viewers could not realistically relate). Narrowing the field of potential texts in such a manner enabled me to focus on the episodes most significant to the subjects examined in this study – Scully, Gillian Anderson, and female fans. This further scrutiny yielded a handful of episodes, from which I chose two: "The Pilot" from season one (original airdate September 10, 1993) and "Memento Mori" from season four (original airdate February 9, 1997). While two discrete shows do not constitute a representative sample of *The X-Files*, each episode does reflect a faithful depiction of the Scully character as exemplified in the series. Gillian Anderson concurs that these particular installments were "definitely turning points" for the character of Scully and for herself as actor (Gillian Anderson, personal interview, March 3, 2002).

"The Pilot" is where groundwork for the series is laid and principal characters Fox Mulder and Dana Scully are established as special agents in the Federal Bureau of Investigation. This inaugural episode is also significant to Gillian Anderson in that it served as her foray into steady television work and certainly into popular culture appeal. Second is "Memento Mori," which aired during the pinnacle season of the series. Gillian Anderson earned an Emmy Award for Outstanding Lead Actress in a Drama Series, as well as Golden Globe and Screen Actors Guild top honors, for her intimately personal portrayal of Scully coping with the diagnosis of terminal cancer in this exceptional episode.

I reviewed the selected episodes several times with the goal of identifying and analyzing the challenges confronting Scully and how she achieves resolution. Ultimately, I strove to uncover themes provocative for what they inform about challenges faced by women in contemporary American culture, and to elucidate how a fictional role model serves as an encouraging example to women. Per standard procedures of textual analysis, critical attention was paid to plot, dialogue, agency, symbolism, and closure. Because media texts are polysemic, undoubtedly a variety of readings could be produced from these stories, some of which position Scully as victim. However, since the vast majority of research data acclaim this female character as constructive in the lives of women, I chose to expound her positive qualities.

Historical Treatment of Popular Press Discourse

Following analysis of the textual implications of Scully as role model, I next establish and describe the body of press discourse on Gillian Anderson in an effort to demonstrate how she, the real person, is constructed as a role model through popular culture mechanisms. Richard Dyer (1979) refers to the constructed persona of celebrities as "star image," which he defines as consisting of "media texts that can be grouped together as promotion, publicity, films, and criticism and commentary" (p. 60). The majority of media texts he lists are essentially funneled through the popular press apparatus, given that it constitutes the arena where most information on stars is made publicly available. Consequently, my own analysis does not distinguish whether individual articles on Gillian Anderson are intended to promote, publicize, criticize, or comment (to the extent that could even be determined); rather, it focuses on how her image is framed by the whole of popular press discourse.

In accordance with principles of qualitative inquiry, the data for this component of the project was culled from a variety of print and Internet sources, covering the years 1993 through 2003. Much of the data I found relative to Gillian Anderson I first learned of through the Official Gillian Anderson Website, to whose site administrators I am greatly indebted. I also conducted my own searches in several academic databases and on the Internet using the Google search engine. The bulk of material accumulated on Gillian Anderson, consisting mainly of interviews and celebrity reports, derived from popular magazine and newspaper articles and from entertainment news websites. Each bit of source material was photocopied or printed for review and categorization. My effort to collect most anything I could find resulted in a substantial amount of data that required extensive cataloging. In order to ascertain the possibilities and particulars of this express discourse, I separated the material into a number of topic areas predicated on the frequency with which they appeared. These included what journalists said about Gillian Anderson in terms of the X-Files series and the Scully character as well as accounts of her personal life. This exercise was not as straightforward as it may seem since most all the data is presented in the form of interviews with Gillian Anderson, consequently allowing little room for the voice of the writer to come through. Usually, such perspective was procured from the introduction of articles where some context was provided prior to the requisite question and answer segment. From here I assembled a salient set of subjects that formed a reasonable framework of press discourse on Gillian Anderson as it relates to her position of role model. Specifically, my analysis elaborates on the conflation of the person of Gillian Anderson with the character of Scully; the groundbreaking nature of Scully as a role model for women; and aspects of Gillian Anderson distinct from Scully, including her celebrity status, social activism, and acting career. Though assessing how Gillian Anderson's image was framed by the popular press during the time she starred in *The X-Files*, I recognize that the natural fluidity of any circulating discourse precludes it from ever "fixing" a star's cultural legitimacy. The popular discourse on Gillian Anderson has inevitably shifted since *The X-Files* series ended in 2002, and will continue to shift as her celebrity placement within popular culture fluctuates over time.

Voice of Gillian Anderson

In regard to studying the media, Tulloch (1990) asserts, "the importance of ethnographic analysis is in its taking human actors' (whether 'performers' or 'audience') self-understandings seriously" (p. 20). Without a doubt, an invaluable contribution to this research endeavor is the voice of Gillian Anderson. Through numerous print and broadcast interviews published over the course of a decade, Ms. Anderson has shared personal aspects of what it means to play the character of Scully and how she as actor operates within the broader context of the entertainment industry. In addition to these resources, I am fortunate to have had opportunity to speak with Ms. Anderson personally about her experience as a celebrity role model. My review of Gillian Anderson's own words – on Scully, fans, activism, and her career – seeks to answer the question of how she negotiates her position *with* a role model (Scully) and also *as* a role model herself. Gillian Anderson, the person, is foundational to the role model construct and rightly necessitates equal consideration alongside the textual manifestation of Scully, popular press discourse on her celebrity image, and fan responses to them both.

Inspired by Kathleen Rowe's (1995) exhortation to go "straight to the source" (p. 56), as she did in her treatment of the comedian Roseanne, I pursued an interview with the subject of my own study, Gillian Anderson. In March 2000, I faxed an interview request letter to Gillian Anderson's manager that identified my status as a graduate student and briefly explained my research interests involving feminist media theory and televisual representations of women role models. I defined what I hoped to learn from an interview with Ms. Anderson and stated that, although information from our conversation would not appear in the popular press, it would at least be made available to the academic community. I was surprised when, four days later, an assistant to Ms. Anderson's manager contacted me to tentatively accept my request for an interview. I initiated contact several times over the next few weeks in order to set a firm date, and was informed each time that Ms. Anderson's busy calendar precluded her from scheduling a time for us to talk. Having attempted and failed repeatedly to secure an interview, I eventually suspended my appeal.

In January 2002, I faxed a second interview request letter to Ms. Anderson's manager. I was again surprised when her manager's assistant called two days later to set up a telephone interview within the week. I had continued to work on my project in the intervening two years and, by now, had collected and reviewed hundreds of interviews given by Ms. Anderson. These consisted primarily of popular magazine articles, newspaper pieces, and television appearances. In reading print interviews, I noted generic questions that she had been asked multiple times so that I could avoid asking them of her again. While watching televised interviews, I observed her reactions to types of questions and how they were posed so as to determine her interviewing preferences. The many hours I devoted to this research was well worth the effort as it facilitated a smooth and illuminating dialogue with Ms. Anderson.

On the afternoon of February 20, 2002, Ms. Anderson phoned me at the appointed time. As required by law, I asked if I could record the interview, to which she agreed. I then read a short script informing her that the interview will be used for educational purposes and requesting consent for her name to be associated with my thesis project on role models, to which she also agreed. However, after posing my first question, Ms. Anderson asked if the interview could be rescheduled until a time when she felt better prepared to discuss the subject, explaining, "I don't have much to say on the topic today, but I want to do this with you" (Gillian Anderson, personal interview, February 20, 2002). The next time we spoke was March 3, 2002, when Ms. Anderson called again in order to resume the interview. Generously granting me

30 minutes of her time that Sunday afternoon, she was clearly thoughtful and deliberate in her responses to the questions I posed. (See Appendix A for the list of interview questions).

The transcribed version of our interview serves as the primary data source for my discussion on the negotiation processes of Gillian Anderson. Constituting secondary source materials are statements she has made in popular magazine and newspaper articles, televised publicity appearances, entertainment news websites, online chats, personal messages to fans, and speeches presented at industry award ceremonies and charity events. Similar to obtaining data related to popular press discourse, I gathered this information from print and Internet sources over the course of three years. Such an extensive assortment of material on the person of Gillian Anderson provided the means for a thorough analysis on how she negotiates her position of celebrity role model.

Practices of Female Fans

Upon analyzing how Scully and Gillian Anderson are constructed as role models via the text and popular press discourse, and the ways Gillian Anderson negotiates her own unique position, the final component to be explored is the negotiation processes of female fans; specifically, extra-cinematic identificatory practices. In talking about fandom, Grossberg (1992) writes, "People are constantly struggling, not merely to figure out what a text means, but to make it mean something that connects to their own lives, experiences, needs and desires" (p. 52). Gaining insight into how fans engage in the "struggle" to negotiate meanings and embrace points of identification with Scully and Gillian Anderson, on both professional and personal levels, is necessary to understanding the degree to which she as role model influences fan activity. I specifically examine what female fans *do* with their knowledge of Scully and Gillian Anderson, and how certain modes of imitative behavior can ultimately benefit realms outside the immediate social context of individual fans. Data on fans was accumulated exclusively through the Internet from fan websites, message boards, and hosted chats. I would have included material from the popular press had it existed. However, even though press accounts regularly reference the enormous fandom surrounding *The X-Files* and its stars, most journalistic stories stop short of interviewing actual fans. The Internet afforded an easily accessible panoramic view of what fans say about Gillian Anderson and about themselves, and the assorted means by which they convey their admiration. It is also the venue where most fundraising efforts spearheaded by her fans are situated.

In order to determine how women engage in role modeling of Scully and Gillian Anderson, I sought out their own voices. I began with two primary websites: the Official Gillian Anderson Website and the Order of the Blessed Saint Scully the Enigmatic. Links from these websites to other popular fan-related websites expanded the number of Internet data sources to approximately ten, providing additional opportunities for me to examine a variety of personal stories. While the quantity of information available online is vast, and I certainly could have drawn from hundreds of sources, I relied on a controllable set of high-volume, respected websites that typically hosted message boards. Within this virtual sphere of fandom, I further limited my study to message posts, bulletin board discussions, and activities that directly related to Scully and Gillian Anderson as role models. Since my goal is to examine the cultural construct of celebrity role modeling, I was more interested in distinguishing types of fan *activity* performed during the process of negotiation than I was in dissecting types of fan subcultures (e.g., fan fiction writers, analytical newsgroups). My method for data gathering primarily entailed perusing fan message boards on a regular basis from 2000 to 2003. The forms of fan experiences I encountered were diverse, ranging from people who dyed their hair red in honor of Scully to those who undertook the enormous responsibility of organizing fundraising campaigns to benefit Gillian Anderson's favored causes. I next categorized the data into two broad types of identificatory practices: 1) what fans *say* to and about Gillian Anderson, and 2) what fans *do* in honor of Gillian Anderson. I give cursory treatment to what fans say in preference to what fans do in order to achieve my objective of demonstrating how individual identification with, and imitation of, role models can ultimately benefit society at large.

Because it is not imperative to this analysis, I omit most personal identifying information when excerpting portions of posts and chats. I do, however, note names of websites as well as who maintains them when applicable to the discussion. I make assumptions as to the gender of online fans based on how they self-identify, acknowledging that it is impossible to positively determine gender inasmuch as the Internet is a virtual, rather than an actual, environment. I attempt to use as examples those fans who post under clearly female-oriented online names or have otherwise identified themselves as female, such as with a picture.

In his writing on the intertextuality of television, John Fiske (1987) defines tertiary texts as "the texts that the viewers make themselves out of their responses, which circulate orally or in letters to the press. These third-level texts form much of the data for the ethnographic study of audiences. ... Studying them can give us insights into how the primary [e.g., the television series] and secondary [e.g., press coverage] texts are read and circulated in the culture of viewers" (p. 124). I approached the online fan discourse as tertiary text, gleaning meaning from fans' own words and actions relayed publicly via computer-mediated-communication. While a deeper understanding of particular women's engagement with Scully and Gillian Anderson could have been obtained through in-depth interviewing, I preferred to interpret fans' naturally occurring articulations and actions. Indeed, inconspicuous observation of women's practices of identification and imitative behavior renders an honest account of how they negotiate Scully and Gillian Anderson as role models.

Limitations of the Study

To examine text, context, production, and audience by way of a 202-episode television series, copious popular press discourse covering ten years, hundreds of celebrity interviews during that same period, and a worldwide fan base is admittedly too large of an enterprise to tackle within the parameters of this study. Nevertheless, I did attempt to keep the project manageable and the analysis relevant by choosing very carefully the precise components to study within each subject area and elaborating on each in light of the others.

Limitations specific to the textual analysis are that, of the approximately 30 episodes which center on Scully, just two are reviewed. Although they still sufficiently convey Scully's position as a role model for women, analysis of additional episodes could have provided a more comprehensive rendering. For the examination of circulating discourses on Gillian Anderson, my original intent was actually nearer a broader socio-historical discussion of her popular culture presence. When that avenue proved too unwieldy given the parameters of this project, I narrowed my focus to an examination of just popular press discourse which, by itself, generated a vast amount of material. Considering the multiple themes I uncovered, a number of germane issues were unavoidably omitted. As to Gillian Anderson the actor, here I feel the most inclusive analysis was performed. This estimation is warranted in view of the personal interview I was able to obtain combined with my extensive review of most all other interviews she has given over the past ten years. Contrasted to the level of attention I was able to give Gillian Anderson is the more narrow treatment that could be afforded her fans. Fandom is a complex phenomenon that must be examined at certain junctures in order to arrive at a constructive understanding of its cultural import. The study might have benefited from a more in-depth investigation of fan message boards on what women say in regard to their affection for Scully and Gillian Anderson; on the other hand, such an approach could have put a disproportionate emphasis on the fan component. Ultimately, for what I was able to examine relevant to this project, I believe the end product accurately depicts the cultural construct of a celebrity role model.

Structure of Analysis

Through this qualitative study on the enduring images of Scully and Gillian Anderson of *The X-Files*, I attempt to offer an original conceptualization of the celebrity role model construct. This is accomplished by fairly equally considering elements of text, context, star, and fans. Based on the methods heretofore described, these four elements are developed over the following two chapters. Chapter Five addresses the first research question concerning how Scully and Gillian Anderson are constructed as role models for women. The first half of the chapter deals with Scully in *The X-Files* text and the second half examines popular press discourse on Gillian Anderson. These two issues are combined in one question and in one chapter because they both work to *frame* how Scully/Gillian Anderson is constructed as a popular culture role model. As directed in the second and third research questions, Chapter Six delves the *negotiation* processes of the primary subjects that are affected by the text and press discourse – Gillian Anderson and fans. The first half of the chapter focuses on Gillian Anderson's personal experience of being a role model for women within the context of stardom, while the second half explores specific facets of fan identificatory practices.

CHAPTER V

FRAMING A CELEBRITY ROLE MODEL

Scully in *The X-Files* Text

> Whatever you've found or whatever you might find – I think that we both
> know that right now the truth is in me, and that's where I need to pursue it, as
> soon as possible (Scully in "Memento Mori").

The truth that Scully and Mulder seek may very well be *in* Scully, but

discovering any absolute truth *about* Scully is less likely. The polysemic structure of

television texts assures that the character of Scully, operating on both an individual

level and within the larger episodic and series narratives, can be read myriad ways.

Viewers interpret her by referencing their own socio-historic circumstances and

unique cultural knowledge, and through the negotiation process thereby confer

particular meaning to certain behaviors and experiences of Scully. Some may read

her as a stereotypical female victim, while others see her as an unconventional role

model for women. Academic scholars who write about *The X-Files* usefully

demonstrate the range of differences in understanding Scully. For example, Inness

(1999) sees the character as representative of patriarchal Hollywood's containment of

tough women, observing, "Scully is captured by the killer and needs to be rescued by

Mulder; rarely is this scenario reversed, with Mulder requiring his partner to rescue

him. Again, these episodes are far from innocent, because they reinforce traditional

ideology that men are the ones who are the heroes, not women" (p. 99). Quite the

opposite, Wilcox and Williams (1996) stress, "It should be noted that in *The X-Files*,

there is no overriding pattern of Scully as the damsel in distress. Sometimes Scully

rescues Mulder; sometimes Mulder rescues Scully…. [T]he first partner to do the

saving is Scully in "Deep Throat," the second episode of the series" (p. 109), inferring

perhaps Scully edges Mulder in heroic effort. The straightforward question of how

many times Scully saves or is saved by Mulder can be reasonably resolved through

content analysis, but, barring this formulaic avenue of inquiry, the significant point here is that Inness and Wilcox and Williams offer very different interpretations of how Scully functions in the narrative. Viewers and the popular press likewise perceive Scully differently from each other and from academics, although the clear pattern among the first two audiences is to interpret Scully as a role model.

This preamble is not intended to undermine the conclusions of the forthcoming textual analysis; rather, it is meant to illustrate there is no one specific truth that can be had about a character or a text. Academics and average viewers alike interpret Scully from various points-of-view, which necessarily results in various readings of the character. Because most scholarship on *The X-Files* tends to critically examine Scully in terms of ideological mechanisms, they consequently locate multiple deficiencies related to her as mediated image of woman. This analysis attempts to counter that tendency by purposely accentuating the positive nature of Scully, as determined from reading the text closer to the surface. In other words, what does the obvious narrative (comprised of plot, dialog, and filmic technique) convey about Scully? It is on this level that viewers, who generally read entertainment less rigorously than do academics, are more likely to interpret the character and make connections between her and their own situations. As Gledhill (1988) notes, "The complete reading – from narrative disruption, to enigma development, to resolution – that arises from repeated viewings and close analysis is the product of the critical profession and does not replicate the 'raw' reading/viewing of audiences" (p. 73).

Ideological analyses are, of course, necessary toward a comprehensive understanding of the character's cultural significance. It is readily acknowledged that Scully does not exist outside of dominant influences, for at times she is certainly disempowered by the narrative, traditionally positioned as victim, and symbolic of how much further women must advance in order to achieve gender parity in American society. Still, the fact that "role model for women" has been the one phrase most often invoked by fans and the popular press to describe Scully calls for a closer examination of what makes her so admirable. Textual readings of two discrete episodes from seasons one and four of *The X-Files* elaborate on the ways in which Scully functions as a popular culture role model. The textual analysis begins with a discussion on the concept of the gaze as it applies to Scully. This is useful in framing the innovation and contradiction inherent to this television character, given that her influence partly stems from the authority she possesses through just such a controlling gaze.

Scully's Gaze

Alluding to how the gaze is operationalized in *The X-Files* text by the Scully character, Badley (2000) contends, "Through her looks (as opposed to her appearance) ...Scully has reversed and traversed female stereotypes" (p. 61). The idea that Scully does the looking, and therefore advancing of the story, runs counter to Mulvey's (1975) theory of an active/male and passive/female structure of filmic discourse, where the male hero is said to control both the erotic gaze and narrative events. It also challenges the standard television formula of compelling-male-hero-is-assisted-by-beautiful-and-dutiful-female-partner. In this text, Scully is granted unusual agency for a woman to *look* at evidence, *look* into human (and alien) bodies, and *look* directly in the eye of countless local and federal male law enforcement officers as she gathers information in the course of solving X-File cases. Borrowing Doane's phrase (as cited in Thornham, 1998), the "active investigating gaze" (p. 219) she employs as a FBI special agent is authentic and empowering. On the other hand, although she does much looking at and into things, seemingly "traversing" female stereotypes in the process, Wilcox and Williams (1996) maintain that "Scully's gaze is disempowered by the text" (p.117), at least in terms of observable paranormal activity. What Mulder and the audience see is oftentimes denied Scully, who routinely arrives on scene too late or is knocked semi-unconscious in some manner and therefore disallowed any reliable vision. (Both of these techniques are used in "The Pilot" to disempower Scully's gaze). The audience is securely positioned to identify with Mulder on account that his gaze is validated by framed looks of the director/camera. But, the (in)ability to see what is being shown the audience is only one component of "gazing," so that it does not necessarily follow that Scully's lack of personal encounters with the paranormal signifies absolute absence of a female gaze. Nor is it indicative that she is the passive image to another's active gaze. In fact, on these two counts the Scully character essentially defies Mulvey's model of the gaze, whereas she does not serve as the eroticized object of Mulder's male gaze *and* that she possesses and demonstrates qualities distinctive of her own determining female gaze.

The primary reason Scully is spared Mulder's admiring gaze is that it is focused elsewhere. The gaze of the lead male character that would theoretically be directed at the lead female character is diverted in this particular televisual text toward the paranormal, which serves as the object of his fascination. Ever watchful and aroused for what is happening "out there," Mulder is unaffected by the femaleness of the woman at his side. Wilcox and Williams (1996) describe Mulder and Scully's uncommon television relationship as one where, "They look into each other's eyes and argue ideas, rather than gazing at each other's bodies" (p. 112). Because of Mulder's redirected gaze, Scully is liberated from serving as a "to-be-looked-at" image for both him and viewers and thus is able to exercise her own active investigating gaze.

Scully's control over the narrative is best illustrated by her dual function as stand-in for the audience and by her regular expressions of rational skepticism at Mulder's eccentric notions. To the extent that Mulder represents the active gaze of viewers for what they *see*, Scully represents the active gaze (or the voice) of viewers for what they might *reason*. The audience may see what Mulder sees, but they identify with what Scully argues. She carries the audience with her intellectually as she challenges Mulder to produce supportable theories on the strange phenomena in which he so strongly believes, posing the questions that must be answered in order for them to make advancements in investigations and be taken seriously by FBI brass. As a discriminating audience would expect of the character meant to function as their representative, Scully is written and acted smartly enough so that her arguments on behalf of scientific veracity are believable and respectable. Scully's influence over the narrative is made manifest as Mulder strives to address the issues she raises which, through a balance of her science and his intuition, eventually leads them closer to the truth they seek.

Insofar that Scully functions in tandem with Mulder, offering along with him valuable input on the cases they undertake and defying stereotypical placement as object to his gaze, she can be said to maintain a degree of control over narrative events. In each episode, Scully is afforded a privileged voice of interpretation that helps determine the ways she and Mulder do business in their capacity as federal investigators of the paranormal. In the movie *Fight the Future* (1998), Mulder acknowledges Scully's critical contribution to the X-Files enterprise when he implores her not to quit their partnership: "As difficult and as frustrating as it's been sometimes, your goddamned strict rationalism and science have saved me a thousand times over. You've kept me honest. You've made me a whole person. I owe you everything, Scully, and you owe me nothing." Clearly, Scully's determining gaze does exists and is absolutely imperative to the grand narrative of *The X-Files*.

Scully as Role Model

It has been established that through mechanisms of the gaze Scully possesses the power to shape narrative events. She may not always prevail, but she nonetheless brings to bear on the text a female agency that is rare for series television (even more so when *The X-Files* debuted in 1993) and one that women viewers, in particular, can appreciate. Scully is also someone with whom women can identify. Not, of course, with her status as a FBI agent specializing in forensic science and working in the supernatural realm; rather, women identify with Scully as a contemporary woman who faces challenges and doubts and who endeavors to achieve a fulfilling life. It is on this fundamental level of human experience that Scully is best understood as a role model. How she deals with universal conditions and events involving professional matters and personal adversity is what provides the grounds for identification and role modeling. Indeed, the crux of Scully's position as role model is located in her authenticity as an independent woman grappling with familiar life issues. Narrative resolution to Scully's struggles may be unique to her fictional circumstances, but the manner in which she conducts herself imparts inspiration to engaged viewers.

The following analysis of two prominent episodes of *The X-Files* is intended to distinguish and elaborate on instances where Scully exhibits traits of a positive role model. The circumstances that confront Scully, how she manages them, and meanings women viewers may extract from her experiences are presented in light of the larger subject of Scully and Gillian Anderson as celebrity role models. "The Pilot" is a crucial episode to examine because it initially frames the character of Special Agent Dana Scully. It is here that she is established as an intelligent, confident, and principled woman. These attributes are certainly not uncommon to women, but one place they are more difficult to come by is in *television* women. When viewers are able to locate a thoroughly competent woman such as Scully on television, the most ubiquitous medium of popular culture, it is reasonable that she would be deemed a role model. The presentation of Scully's compelling story as a FBI agent newly assigned to the X-Files unit is the focus of analysis on "The Pilot." Considered next is "Memento Mori," the tour de force that secured Gillian Anderson the 1997 Emmy, Golden Globe, and Screen Actors' Guild awards for best female actor. As an intimate character study, it provides a different perspective on Scully's strengths than are seen in the first installment. While the series' pilot episode necessarily presents Scully from without – that is, in defining and reinforcing her quintessential qualities – the fourth season mytharc episode "Memento Mori," which translates to "remember that you must die" (Latin), meaningfully reveals her from within. Or, more precisely, it allows Scully to reveal herself through voiceover. Faced with the diagnosis of terminal cancer, Scully's function as a role model is realized by her personal journey of dealing with the implications of this devastating news.

"The Pilot"

The X-Files pilot essentially begins and ends with Scully. Following a teaser that sets up the ensuing mystery, the episode opens with a tracking shot of Agent Scully on her way to a meeting with superiors in the J. Edgar Hoover FBI Building in Washington D.C. Visually, viewers are invited to identify with Scully by striding alongside her as she confidently navigates a maze of desks en route to see the section chief. When the main story closes at the end of the hour, Scully is shown contemplating the ramifications of her continuing work as a FBI special agent. The close-up of her pondering the preceding extraordinary events after a phone conversation with Mulder encourages yet further (and more intimate) identification. These "bookend" shots of Scully yield both a visual and narrative impact, confirming her significance in *The X-Files*.

In terms of narrative relevance, Scully's placement at the head of the text signals her role as storyteller. This position is supported when Scully and viewers, together, learn that the reason for her visit with superiors is for reassignment to the

X-Files unit and then, together, enter a basement office to meet her new partner, Agent Mulder. With the exception of witnessing the episode's climactic paranormal event, the audience is always with Scully – from opening to close. The idea that viewers closely accompany Scully as she maneuvers through "The Pilot" is consistent with executive producer Chris Carter's vision of her serving as the audience's representative. This narrative strategy is yet more apparent considering that Mulder is almost never in a scene without Scully, whereas she is shown immersed in thought and hard at work on several occasions without him. She is given extended screen time as the character charged with leading viewers through a rather complex story. In short, Scully is the narrative touchstone of *The X-Files*.

Upon arriving at her superior's office, Scully is informed that she has been reassigned to work in the X-Files unit with the brilliant though disdained Agent Mulder. She is to assist him on cases and report back her "observations on the validity of the work." In the course of this initial conversation with the section chief it is revealed that Scully was recruited by the FBI directly out of medical school, and that her motivations for joining the Bureau instead of pursuing medicine include a desire to distinguish herself professionally. When Scully meets Mulder for the first time, she defends against his insinuation that she was sent to spy on him by declaring her qualifications and credentials, at which time he interrupts to convey, "You're a medical doctor. You teach at the academy. You did your undergraduate degree in physics." Through encounters with the section chief and Mulder early on in the pilot episode, Scully is immediately marked as highly proficient – a trained doctor and scientist, skilled enough to be hand-picked by the FBI to instruct other agents, and now entrusted to "make the proper scientific analysis" of one gifted agent's work on strange unsolved cases.

In writing on the broadcast industry, Walker and Ferguson (1998) comment that, "Entertainment television provides few role models that seem to derive their status from academic achievement. Even successful professionals (physicians, lawyers, scientists) are seldom shown engaged in study" (p. 175). Scully is one such rare character who defies both of these norms. Her academic knowledge is ever present in the arguments she makes to Mulder on behalf of science. She is furthermore regularly depicted performing autopsies and various medical procedures. Scully's intelligence is articulated in "The Pilot" by frequent scenes of her actively investigating their first case together, which involves alleged alien abduction and murder in a small town along the Oregon coast. She studies the case file on their cross-country flight, asks informed questions of local witnesses, gathers evidence from potential suspects and from the forest where the victim was found, interrogates Mulder for what he already knows, and convinces him of the need to investigate and identify verifiable facts. On more than one occasion, Scully sits in her motel room in the middle of the night typing up her field notes and supplementary analysis on a laptop computer. Scully is additionally shown operating adeptly in her capacity of forensic scientist. Dressed in blue lab attire complete with medical goggles, verbally recording measurement statistics and preliminary observations into an overhead microphone, Scully is clearly in her element autopsying an exhumed corpse. Comparing her to other female television characters, Wilcox and Williams (1996) submit, "while women on screen often passively represent the body, Scully actively examines it" (p. 106-107). Scully's critical analysis – of bodies and of evidence -- is a key trait of the character and the series.

Another indicator of Scully as role model is her confidence. In the important first framing shot of Scully on the way to meet superiors, her deliberate manner of walking exudes a poise and confidence – what Carter refers to as a "certain grounding" – that she maintains throughout the episode. During two meetings with the section chief, Scully is composed and self-assured. She remains so upon meeting Mulder, who straight away tests her medical knowledge and further queries, "Do you believe in the existence of extraterrestrials?" Scully meets his challenge with the retort, "Logically, I would have to say no. ... The answers are there. You just have to know where to look." She is also not timid when, later in the episode, she senses their investigation has been impeded by her partner's refusal to be forthcoming, exclaiming, "Damn it, Mulder, cut the crap! What is going on here?" The reputation of Agent Mulder as both brilliant and bizarre does nothing to inhibit Scully's confidence in herself as an agent or in the science she advocates.

Complementing the qualities of intelligence and confidence fundamental to Scully is an overarching integrity that, from "The Pilot" onward, is the hallmark of her character. Viewers first encounter this integrity when Scully is informed of reassignment by superiors. Stiffening slightly at the directive, she asks, "Am I to understand that you want me to debunk the X-Files project, sir?" Her guarded reaction denotes a sense of suspicion that the section chief's objective in gathering information about Mulder's activities might compromise her professional integrity. Since Mulder is likewise suspicious of the Bureau (and now of Scully), she must assert to him time and again that her intentions are honorable and that she is "not a part of any agenda." When he suggests her purpose in the X-Files may be tied to a larger plan meant to prevent him from exposing covert government operations, she implores him, "You've got to trust me. I'm here just like you, to solve this." Though Scully and Mulder eventually return to Washington D.C. without resolution to the case, having been thwarted in their efforts to retain vital evidence (ostensibly by government operatives), Scully's "dedication to the truth as a doctor and investigator" precludes her from discrediting Mulder as her superiors would have it and consequently hinders her professional advancement (Wilcox and Williams, 1996, p. 103). When the section chief concludes there is "no evidence that justifies the legitimacy of these investigations" and insinuates shutting down the X-Files, Scully presents him with one bit of physical evidence that she has managed to preserve – an implant composed of unidentifiable material pulled from the nasal cavity of the corpse she autopsied. With that, the X-Files project continues. Despite powerful external forces at play, Scully's integrity in the work she does and in her relationship with her partner is beyond compromise.

As presented in "The Pilot," there are several defining characteristics of Scully that make her a good agent, a good person, and a good role model. Perhaps most obviously, Scully is a role model by way of her impressive intelligence. She is a scientist and medical doctor who regularly applies logic and academic training in order to arrive at supportable positions. Scully is also clearly confident and determined in her approach to work. She exudes a self-assuredness that is natural and unpretentious, and which helps to underscore the necessity of employing her scientific methods in investigations. Moreover, she possesses both professional and personal integrity. Scully set a new standard for televisual female role models with her introduction in 1993 – they could be smart, self-confident, and honorable, without being pedantic, arrogant, or sentimental.

<u>"Memento Mori"</u>

"Memento Mori" begins gently with a pure white light that gradually reveals Scully standing alone in a hospital gown and reading an x-ray. The time it takes for the camera to proceed down the passageway of light and finally bring Scully from an indiscernible black dot into mid-shot focus situates viewers for a serious X-File story that revolves around its female lead. Her thoughts are heard in voiceover: "I feel time like a heartbeat, the seconds pumping in my breast like a reckoning. ... I feel the tethers loose and the prospects darken for the continuance of a journey that began not so long ago." Upon being diagnosed with terminal cancer, the episode follows Scully's very personal journey of dealing with impending death as she works through issues involving work, loved ones, treatment options, and hope. The grander narrative discloses that her rare form of brain cancer is the result of abduction and "medical rape" perpetrated three years earlier, and that her involuntary connection to unknown evil forces has left her barren and now dying. Yet within this substantial mythology installment lays an honest account of one woman's experience with cancer.

While Scully stands holding the x-ray confirming cancer, Mulder arrives to learn of the inoperable and virtually untreatable nature of her illness. She tells him calmly, "I have cancer. ... If it pushes into my brain, statistically there is about zero chance of survival." She is succinct and unemotional in relaying the facts of the nasopharengeal mass located between her superior conchea and sinoidal sinus. At this early point, she is only equipped to acknowledge its factual existence from a clinical distance afforded her as a medical doctor. Refusing to accept the inevitability of Scully's death, Mulder embarks on his own journey to find the cause of her cancer in the hopes of finding its cure, which precipitates his spending much of the story away from her. This scenario of Scully and Mulder separated during an extremely sensitive time in her life sets up the episode's most poignant narrative element – the use of voiceover to reveal Scully's innermost thoughts on what it feels like to have terminal cancer. Scully's emotional struggle unfolds primarily through voiceovers of several journal entries written with the intent that Mulder read them after her death, supplemented by key character moments between Scully and another woman dying of the same cancer. The prevalence of cancer in modern society makes it highly probable that most viewers have been touched by its menace in some way or another, perhaps through their own diagnosis or that of a friend or family member. In "Memento Mori," Scully serves as a role model for the inspirational example she provides in dealing with the all too common circumstance of a life-threatening illness.

Early in the episode, Scully and Mulder discover that a group of eleven women they met previously on a case in Allentown, Pennsylvania have nearly all died from the same rare form of brain cancer diagnosed in Scully. The connection shared by these women, besides their illness, is that each claimed similar abduction experiences and found implants in their necks as had Scully. Scully is incredulous at hearing that only one woman of the original group is still alive. A subtle but persistent denial of her condition had kept her from facing the truth that she might eventually die from cancer, making this astonishing information almost too much to process. Scully's response leads Mulder to challenge why she refuses to admit her cancer may be the result of the same sinister plot that has systematically killed the other women. She does not refute Mulder's assertion that she is in denial over her illness, but when he suggests she talk with Penny Northern, the final survivor of the original eleven, she responds with pointed anger: "[Talk] about what? What it feels like to be dying of cancer? What's it's like to know that there's absolutely nothing you can do about it?" After having remained relatively in control up until this point in the narrative, Scully's outburst is startling. Providing points of identification and empathy, the effect of this exchange reminds viewers that she is a woman terrified at the prospect of dying, as any reasonable person would be.

Scully does agree to meet with Penny, who lies dying in the hospital, and soon comes to recognize this woman, ravaged from the effects of chemotherapy and radiation, as symbolic of her own fate. Reconciling herself to the fact that she too faces the same grim future, Scully checks herself into the hospital and begins treatment with the hope that perhaps she will be the one to conquer the disease. Accepting her cancer and deciding to undergo treatment elicits trepidation, as she confesses in her journal: "Mulder, it's difficult to describe to you the fear of facing an enemy which I can neither conquer nor escape." Scully is reassured by Penny, however, who proves to be a friend in giving comfort and understanding following Scully's first dose of chemotherapy. In regard to the extraterrestrial mystery of why so many women have died, Penny encourages Scully to "try to make sense of it. It will help you through the pain to understand why this is happening to you." She refers here to Scully's abduction, but her words also imply that Scully must deal with the "why" of her cancer – to give it meaning in order to gain some control over it and herself. Scully then watches and waits as Penny takes a downturn. Even in her final hours, Penny gives Scully a sense of strength and purpose to carry on, telling her, "Dana, I want you to get well. ... You can't give up hope," to which Scully replies, "I haven't. I won't." Observing before her a woman who did not give up hope, yet who also did not get well, Scully feels a deep respect for Penny and a faith that she too has the "courage to face this journey." Following Penny's death, Scully emerges from her friend's hospital room to find Mulder waiting, having returned from his search with more questions than answers. She tells him that she has decided not to let the cancer beat her. That she will continue to work, to carry on, and to live with cancer – just as people do. Whether the cancer eventually claims her, as it has eleven other women, or not, Scully is resolved to live.

What "Memento Mori" contributes in regard to Scully as a role model is the story of an ordinary woman confronted with a very real disease. No longer is she the "ass-kicking, take-no-shit super scientist" as described by one journalist (Thomas, 2001, para. 3), but a mortal woman not immune to hardship and therefore someone with whom viewers can identify. By the end of the story, Scully has found some clarity and peace in allowing herself to move deliberately through each stage of the process in coming to terms with her cancer, gaining greater self-awareness and strength to persevere. Women facing similar circumstances of struggle (illness or otherwise) may invoke Scully as a mentor, using her example to glean courage as they proceed through various levels of emotion toward resolution of their particular situations. Scully's own process begins with a rational acknowledgment of her condition, and then soon transitions into denial. Once Mulder challenges her, however, she moves into a state of anger over her illness and its ultimate conclusion. This outward wrath masks the underlying terror she feels, as expressed in diary entries to Mulder. Subsequently, the profound encounter Scully has with Penny dissipates her anger and provides a means for her to move into acceptance. Once Scully finally accepts the uncertainty that her future now holds, she is better able to make choices about how she will continue to live her life. The path she takes is individual (and fictional), but it is nonetheless inspirational for those viewers open to its message of courage and determination.

The foregoing textual analysis illuminates two principal features in regard to how the Scully character is framed as a role model. First, she is afforded a privileged voice of interpretation, or narrative authority, which bolsters her cultural legitimacy as a woman to be emulated both professionally and personally. This is established through her position of narrator in "The Pilot," where she serves to represent the gaze/voice of the audience. In "Memento Mori," Scully also narrates, but for a different reason. Here she shares her personal struggle in coping with a deadly disease, advancing the story through voiceovers of journal entries. Secondly, Scully is depicted as actively working through issues on her own, facing difficult situations head-on, and emerging through trials a stronger and wiser person. "The Pilot" clearly shows her determinedly working her first case with Mulder while also handling his resistance to their partnership and the questionable motives of superiors concerning her new assignment. "Memento Mori" turns this resolve inward, as only she can make the journey through the emotional process of coming to terms with her own impending death. Largely consistent throughout *The X-Files'* 202 episodes, the textual elements of Scully as narrator of the story and independent agent of her self combine to form a progressive female television character that women viewers can appreciate and seek to imitate. Still, despite the compelling argument that Scully is exemplary, more than text must be considered when examining the cultural construct of a celebrity role model, for "textual analysis cannot alone determine the progressiveness or otherwise of a particular work" (Gledhill, 1988, p. 74).

Gillian Anderson in Popular Press Discourse

Every so often, magic happens onscreen: Whether through instinct or good fortune, an alchemy occurs and the right actor becomes one with the right role. ... By the end of season two, [Gillian] Anderson had made Dana Scully her own in ways that no one could have anticipated (Perenson, 2000).

Gillian Anderson did not become a celebrity role model through her own making – she was *framed* as a role model by the forces of popular culture; in particular, the popular press. *The X-Files'* character of Scully is indeed a progressive television role model for women, and Gillian Anderson surely does her part in sustaining a respectable reputation, but it is the popular press that basically defines and thereafter shapes her public image, as it attempts to do with all celebrities. Were it not for the substantial and persistent press accounts lauding Scully and Gillian Anderson as role models, neither might have been the enduring popular icons they are today.

Coupled with the preceding textual analysis of Scully in *The X-Files*, a historical treatment of popular press discourse on Gillian Anderson provides a context for examining the negotiation processes of her as a celebrity role model and of fans that engage in identificatory practices based on her image (as considered in the next chapter). The discussion here necessarily begins at Scully since she is the one who first caught the attention of the press. The subtle conflation of Gillian Anderson with Scully and the groundbreaking nature of the Scully character strongly influence how Gillian Anderson is framed for popular culture consumption. Three major discourses circulating within the framework of press coverage on aspects of Gillian Anderson distinct from Scully include her popular status as a celebrity, her personal contributions as a social activist, and her professional career as an actor. The order of the forthcoming analysis essentially charts the evolvement of press discourse which, after starting with a focus on Scully, quickly transitioned to infatuation with the celebrity of Gillian Anderson, occasionally acknowledged her charitable activities, and finally recognized her talents beyond *The X-Files*.

It should be remembered that, for the most part, the popular press does not function to provide thoughtful analysis; rather, it serves more as purveyor of superficial details of the stars it features. It is driven by economic objectives, and as long as stars remain bankable commodities – that is, their pictures and stories sell magazines – the press will continue to write about them in ways that maintain reader interest. These ways entail descriptions of what stars wear, how they act, who they love, where they vacation, and why they think audiences should see their latest film. Contrary to what the popular press purports to convey about celebrities, such information does not impart any *genuine* knowledge about its subjects, according to Richard Dyer (1979), who argues, "we are dealing with stars in terms of their signification, not with them as real people" (p. 2). Regardless of whether interviewers or readers are actually able to glimpse the authentic star or simply what they signify, the popular press at least affords opportunity for learning *something* about celebrities. And this something helps frame how the public comes to know and understand their favored stars.

Conflation of Disparate Star Images

It is obvious that Gillian Anderson and Dana Scully are different people. Aside from the fact one is authentic and one is fictional, they each have very different backgrounds, educational experiences, professions, and perspectives. However, distinguishing between real and imaginary images does not hinder the popular press from attempting to construct the image of the star on the foundation of the character. Fans come to their favored stars through favored characters, augmenting their intimate knowledge of what they see on television with what they read in celebrity magazines. By purposely keeping stars closely connected to their characters, even years after a successful series ends, the press is able to sustain a healthy degree of reader interest and hence profit.

When *The X-Files* began, nearly all focus in regard to its female lead was understandably on the Scully character, with early press accounts speaking first to Scully's status as role model and second to Gillian Anderson as the actor who portrayed her. As public interest in *The X-Files'* swelled, attention shifted to the stars of the show, Gillian Anderson and David Duchovny, both of whom had been little known prior to their roles of Scully and Mulder. Along with this normal transition in emphasis from characters to actors came a conflation of the image of Gillian Anderson with the image of Scully. The steady undercurrent of parallels drawn by the press between these dual images had the effect of one being interpreted in direct relation to the other. Blurring their differences more often than not resulted in the person of Gillian Anderson being read in light of the character of Dana Scully.

Perhaps because Gillian Anderson was a virtual unknown to both the press and the public prior to her foray into series television, early on some journalists were inclined to base their conceptions of Gillian Anderson on what they knew of Scully, at times writing about them as if their characteristics were interchangeable. One journalist even suggests the two women are more similar than the actor herself realizes, "Anderson – strong, intelligent, hard working, and passionate about her work – has more in common with Scully than she thinks" (Melcombe, 1995, para. 22). Despite this example of overt conflation, the most common method employed by the popular press to link images of Gillian Anderson and Scully entails comparing and contrasting actor and character. For example, Gillian Anderson has been routinely asked in interview settings about her belief in the paranormal and how she resembles Scully in various respects. Her responses generally make clear there are significant differences between herself and the character. However, the mere fact that she speaks of Scully on a relatively personal level and in reference to herself actually works to reinforce the correlation of the two images in the eyes of the public.

The popular press' initial framing of Gillian Anderson in relation to Scully diminished as Gillian Anderson, the fast rising star, became central to the discourse and the public became more absorbed in the actor's real life over the character's fictional one. With her rebellious past, "big break" Hollywood story, and propensity for frankness in interviews, she surely proved to be a much more intriguing subject to write about than was Scully. Even so, the formative conflation of Gillian Anderson with Scully persisted, albeit subtly, occasionally prompting a reflective writer to address the question of which celebrated image the press and public was actually most enamored of: "Gillian Anderson...fast became the woman every woman wanted to be. Attractive without being a sex object, brainy without being geeky, fearless without being foolhardy. ... But, then again, who can say if it's Gillian we all respect or her character Dana Scully?" ("The truth is in here," 1999).

Groundbreaking Role Model

When Scully first emerged onto the television landscape of the early 1990s, she marked a turning point for how lead female characters were portrayed and perceived. She was a *thinking* woman in a man's world, equipped by writers to operate from a position of conviction and courage rather than from stereotypical female modes of emotion and vulnerability. The popular press rapidly recognized the uniqueness of the Scully character and framed her from the outset as "groundbreaking." Reviews written during *The X-Files'* first season include pronouncements such as, "She's helped prove that a television role that allows a woman to be smart, professional, and the equal of her male partner does exist" ("Surprise aura of success," 1994, para. 2); and, "Unlike most women paired with male characters in TV series, Anderson's character is very much her own person, able to generate answers and solutions in a coolly professional manner. ... Neither half is superior; neither half less capable in his or her field" (Durden, 1994, para. 10). These particular examples of praise draw attention to one of the realities of women sharing top billing with men in dramatic television; that is, they are seldom represented as being independent competent people. When compared with their male counterparts, women characters are oftentimes depicted in some way as less intelligent, less professional, and/or less in control.

A further implication of these early press reports concerns the revolutionary nature of a female character like Scully on network television. The reason women are given short shrift in leading roles has much to do with the patriarchal Hollywood apparatus and its dominant rendering of gender stereotypes. Scully does not fit the successful (and conventional) formula of female-subordinate-serves-male-superior; rather, she is stationed on equal footing with Mulder, especially in regard to intellectual aptitude. The idea of such a bold female character is a risky concept for television. Any failure on the part of Scully and *The X-Files* to succeed could have constituted a setback for further "existence" of television women who could be considered "very much her own person." Special Agent Dana Scully did succeed, brilliantly, and through credible characterization of positive attributes she set the standard for a new kind of female role model. Her disruption of the Hollywood hegemonic norm caused a stir in the popular press that did not diminish over the lifespan of *The X-Files* series:

1995: "There are very few role models for young women in today's movies and TV shows, and yet...Dana Scully is a woman of strength and intelligence" (Strachan, 1995, para. 8).

1996: "Scully is not only regarded as the stronger of the pair – constantly shooting down Mulder's boy-scout alien theories – she's also regarded as one of the best role models on TV for women" (Barker, 1996).

1997: "She is not the typical 'chick partner,' that delicately fragile and temperamental creature given to highly strung yapping whenever trouble arises" (Saddy, 1997).

1998: "It's that special panache – brainy, skeptical, stone-facedly self-controlled – that makes FBI agent Dana Scully one of television's most fascinating and groundbreaking characters" (Strauss, 1998, para. 3).

1999: Scully is "perhaps the most progressive female character on mainstream TV" (Leith, 1999, para. 1).

2000: Scully represents "unflappable poise" (Lim, 2000, para. 4).

2001: "Scully is still the coolest woman on television" (Thomas, 2001).

It is not only significant that the popular press took notice and aptly acknowledged the innovative contribution of a primetime character like Scully, but that it kept up its praise for the entire nine seasons she was on the air. The amount of positive coverage bestowed on this one television character is extraordinary, undoubtedly doing much to solidify in the minds of audiences her absolute tenure as a role model. One explanation for why the press never lost its fondness for Scully is because they recognized her as a cultural phenom who was paving the way for other television women. In addition to being a groundbreaking leading female character, Scully was placed within the context of a superbly produced show that women and men alike could appreciate. Granted, Scully is not the only pioneer when it comes to progressive television role models for women (consider, for example, Mrs. Peel of *The Avengers*, Jamie Sommers of *The Bionic Woman*, and, notably, Christine Cagney and Mary Beth Lacey of *Cagney & Lacey*). But what she had in her favor over these other television women was the fortune of coming onto the scene at a time when the technological advancement of the Internet, generalized cynicism about government, and the escalation of "postfeminist" debates present in American culture throughout the 1990s coalesced to produce the ideal occasion for a female character such as Scully to capture the public's imagination. With this affection for Scully came immense interest in the woman who embodied her, Gillian Anderson, who by being inextricably identified with Scully, the role model, likewise came to be perceived as a role model.

Aspects of Gillian Anderson

Scully is most certainly considered a role model for women, especially when popular press coverage of the character is taken into account, as illustrated above. But Gillian Anderson, the real woman, is obviously a different kind of role model than is her fictional counterpart. Since she is not a forensic scientist or medical doctor or federal agent, she must be framed otherwise in order to still be deemed a woman worthy of emulation. Without completely detaching her actual image from the venerated image of her character, the popular press frames Gillian Anderson for public consumption in several distinct ways. Foremost, Gillian Anderson is presented as a celebrity, with particular interest placed on her physical attractiveness. These accounts are abundant, far outweighing coverage of her other aspects. By this measure, she is conferred her role model status simply by virtue of being a celebrity. To a much lesser extent (but truer to the nature of a role model) the popular press covers Gillian Anderson as a social activist. Because she is a celebrity, she is afforded the privilege of media attention whenever she takes a prominent role in advancing social and/or political issues. While the press does not accentuate this aspect of her life, its coverage does authenticate Gillian Anderson as a moral role model. A third important way the popular press frames Gillian Anderson is by highlighting her talents as an actor. The dedication with which she performs her work, and the accolades she continues to receive for her efforts, combine to form an exemplar of professional success. Taken together, the ways in which the popular press frames Gillian Anderson as a role model encompass popular, personal, and professional aspects of her person.

Celebrity Popularity

Burgeoning popular interest in *The X-Files* triggered extensive press coverage of the series and its stars. Gillian Anderson and David Duchovny both quickly became mega-celebrities as a result of the popular press' efforts to capitalize on a cult-turned-mainstream-hit television show. After having helped establish Gillian Anderson as a celebrity, the press perpetuated her celebrity status by way of constant coverage. Her position was marked most dramatically by the rash of magazine covers on which she appeared during the height of *X-Files* popularity. Immediately prior to theatrical release of *The X-Files: Fight the Future* in June 1998, Gillian Anderson was featured (oftentimes with her co-star) in cover stories by *Vanity Fair*, *Newsweek*, *Details*, *TV Guide*, *Entertainment Weekly*, *InStyle*, *Yahoo! Internet Life* and *Movieline*, among others. During this same time, reports on the number of reports even appeared, such as one announcing that "Gillian Anderson was splashed across more magazine covers than supermodel Cindy Crawford" (Smith, 2000, para. 6).

Celebrities featured on covers of popular publications are, with few exceptions, portrayed at their most beautiful. Accordingly, Gillian Anderson's adorned face and alluring body was everywhere for a time, on magazine covers and in photo spreads. In 1997, she was among *People* magazine's "50 Most Beautiful People in the World." She was furthermore voted in various polls, both online and those sponsored by men's magazines, as one of the sexiest celebrities alive, including being named *FHM*'s sexist woman of 1996 (and remaining on the list of top 100 sexiest women for six additional years). In announcing Gillian Anderson as its winner, *FHM* called her the "icily cool but unfeasibly sexy Agent Dana Scully" whose sexist moment consisted of her "getting out of that suit for the...photoshoot" (Syson, 1996). Gillian Anderson's celebrity appeal was galvanized by some viewers' need to see a sexualized side of Scully which is largely absent in *The X-Files*. One journalist observes, "Aside from a brief flash of lingerie in the pilot, Scully has been among the most modest of TV characters" (O'Hare, 2002, para. 7).

While Scully is most definitely considered a role model for such estimable attributes as integrity, fortitude, and enlightenment, Gillian Anderson, via the celebrity system, is hailed a role model for her fame, beauty, and desirability. These qualities, though reasonable for wanting to attain, are nonetheless superficial. The fact that Gillian Anderson's own popularity has waned in the years since the end of *The X-Files* is a testament that celebrity status is fleeting and that actors who remain as lasting role models, as she has, do so by exemplifying personal causes and professional accomplishments.

Social Activism

    While the Scully character, to the extent that she is a strong woman, and the popular press, in its fashioning of her persona into a celebrity, afford Gillian Anderson a great deal of renown as a role model, they are ultimately fictionalized and finite constructions that operate outside of her control. It is through social activism that Gillian Anderson is able to distinguish herself apart from these externally-constructed texts and make conscious choices about how she *personally* functions as a role model. Although she is frequently involved in certain nonprofit organizations, popular press coverage of her efforts on behalf of causes is far less extensive than that of issues pertaining to her "celebritydom." Nevertheless, as political consultant Donna Bojarsky states, "when [actors] go to an event, it gets covered" (Adato, 2000, p. 72). Showing Gillian Anderson actively supporting honorable causes with her time and money lends credence to her role model status while also making her more accessible to viewers as a "down-to-earth" person with whom they can identify.

    The amount of space allotted by the popular press to Gillian Anderson in her function as social activist depends on the nature of the publication in which these stories are featured. Additionally, each periodical highlights facets of her philanthropy specific to the interests of its readership, ranging in coverage from the negligible to the substantive. Regardless of article length, however, the fact that the press acknowledges her altruism at all likely influences how audiences perceive Gillian Anderson as well as the entities she aids. Following is a brief examination of three magazine articles that illustrates how Gillian Anderson is constructed as a role model by the press in terms of her social activism.

    A snippet in *People* magazine on Gillian Anderson's financial contribution to a South African youth orchestra for travel to the United States begins, "From the X-File marked 'Good Deeds'" ("Bravo for Anderson," 2001, p. 20). The few sentences that follow provide no context whatsoever about the orchestra or why Gillian Anderson is interested in their organization. In fact, readers are really meant to identify with the last line that comments on the music director's initial assumption of her benefactor being a struggling actor: "The truth, of course, was out there – her students filled her in." For *People*, the fact that Gillian Anderson assisted a group of young musicians with touring expenses is beside the point; instead, it is meant to convey that kids as far away as South Africa know who she is because of her celebrity status. Despite this shallow angle, the piece is notable for its framing of Gillian Anderson as an admirable woman who helps a worthy cause. The article further manages to specify the group, thus affording some measure of publicity for the Buskaid Soweto String Project and of Gillian Anderson as their sponsor.

A slightly more fleshed-out account of Gillian Anderson's commitment to social issues is demonstrated by *InStyle*, a celebrity-focused magazine marketed to women. In an article on ten young female stars who "jump at the chance to share their idol thoughts" (Morrison, 2000), readers are positioned to identify with the featured celebrities who, just like them, are starstruck. Described as a "cerebral sex symbol, single mom and Emmy winner," Gillian Anderson is presented beside her idol, author and children's rights advocate Marian Wright Edelman. She is quoted as being inspired by Wright Edelman to "get up off [her] butt" and become involved in Neurofibromatosis, Inc., to the point of speaking before members of Congress in support of increased research funding for the disorder that has been diagnosed in her younger brother. Similar to *People*, *InStyle* is not particularly interested in elaborating on the benevolence of Gillian Anderson (or on the merits of Wright Edelman's important work, for that matter); however, the article succinctly captures a number of ways in which readers can distinguish her as a role model. She is described as intelligent, sexy, loyal, and compassionate in conjunction with the more ordinary state of being a fan, single mother, and professional career woman – all of which provide points of identification for her fans and effectively result in Gillian Anderson emerging as more the role model than the woman she admires.

The final article considered, featured in the April 2000 edition of *George*, explicitly addresses the social activism of Gillian Anderson among several other celebrities, including Bono, Susan Sarandon, and Barbra Streisand. The "Save the World Awards" highlights Gillian Anderson's involvement with the Feminist Majority Foundation as a spokesperson during its campaign against California's 1996 anti-affirmative action initiative, along with mention of her more personal fundraising efforts on behalf of Neurofibromatosis, Inc. Significantly, the piece directly links Gillian Anderson's authentic social interests to her fictional role of Scully and the adoring female fans she engenders by noting, "She – or, at least, the character she portrays – was already inspiring viewers. ... Her fan base, and her own passions, made her a natural match to the Feminist Majority Foundation" (Adato, 2000, p. 60). This deliberate conflation of the inspirational nature of Scully with the social concerns of Gillian Anderson not only reinforces their dual images as role models, but effectively credits fans as well for motivating her feminist activism.

Transcending Scully

In examining popular press accounts of Gillian Anderson in her capacity of professional actor, it becomes clear she is highly valued for her performance. The aspect of Gillian Anderson as a role model here stems from two points made by the press in regard to her acting ability – one, that she is the perfect embodiment of Scully and, two, that she possesses talent far beyond what she could feasibly reveal through Scully. Gillian Anderson worked as an actor before being cast as Scully, before becoming a celebrity, and before undertaking charitable causes. As her profession, acting is what most defines her person (outside of family), which is why she must transcend the confines of Scully if she is to continue her career. The same wonderful character that sped her meteoric rise to stardom could just as readily imprison her in a permanent state of stereotypical Scully-esque roles. For the nine years that *The X-Files* was produced, Gillian Anderson endeavored to perform Scully consistently well and was rewarded several industry honors for her efforts. During brief hiatus periods and after the series ended, she worked doubly hard to move past the character with whom her name had become synonymous. Her own efforts notwithstanding, the popular press still holds a tremendous amount of sway in how she is perceived by the public and, by extension, in her level of success as an actor.

FOX network executives had not been convinced Gillian Anderson was the best woman to play Scully, and throughout much of the first season kept open the option of replacing her. But the popular press was on her side, as illustrated by a review declaring, "by mid-season (if not earlier), it was obvious she was perfect for the role. With Anderson at the helm, Scully is smart, resourceful, and strong" (Miller, 1994, para. 4). Over the course of the show, other journalists would assert that she is "the glue that holds *The X-Files* together" (Strachan, 1995, para. 7); is "as vital to *The X-Files* health as the show has been to her career" (Strauss, 1998, Star wars section, para. 5); and "helped turn Scully from a mere sidekick to one of TV's leading ladies" (Avalos and Liedtke, 2000, para. 11). Many more accounts specifically credit Gillian Anderson for the success of the Scully character and, occasionally, the series itself. These subtle reminders that Gillian Anderson was responsible to a great extent for *The X-Files*' popularity certainly validate her hiring, but they also solidify her reputation as a talented actor. Owing to press coverage, she is presented as a role model for the exceptional abilities she brings to her craft and for garnering industry accolades in recognition of her work. Viewers, not the least among them aspiring actors, doubtless glean inspiration and motivation from Gillian Anderson based on the glowing reports of her success.

Gillian Anderson flourished in the television role of Scully, in part due to protracted support of the press. However, she had no intention of continuing in the medium at the close of *The X-Files*; rather, she aspired to work in film. In order for her to transcend the boundaries of the small screen world she inhabited for nearly a decade, it would be extremely valuable for the popular and critical press to also lend support for her transition to the big screen. Fortunately for Gillian Anderson, the press, which aided her career firstly by supporting her casting as Scully, subsequently praised her film portrayals of other characters. Performances in supporting roles in *Chicago Cab* (1998), *The Mighty* (1998), and *Playing By Heart* (1999) were met with acceptance and approval, though coverage was limited in view of her playing relatively minor characters in modest films.

Although *The X-Files* did not end until 2002, Gillian Anderson found time in the summer of 1999 to finally star in a small independent film titled *The House of Mirth* (2000), an adaptation of the book by Edith Wharton. Her exquisite portrayal of doomed society heroine Lily Bart caught the press off-guard, which illustrates the second avenue of acclaim for her as a model professional actor. That is, her distinction as a role model no longer relied on a connection to Scully, but was now apparent in other aspects of her career. The press even expounded on its own surprise at her ability to so deftly assume a movie role apart from Scully, as exemplified in *Film Review*: "Merely saying she rises to the occasion with a brilliance *The X-Files* has hardly ever hinted at is an understatement. ...[H]er range is astonishing..." (Jones, 2000). Addressing the potential of Gillian Anderson to surpass Scully and achieve success as a film actor, another journalist proclaims, "For its depth and nuance, this is the kind of classic performance that we once would have expected from someone like Bette Davis or Glenda Jackson. Certainly it shows us that Agent Scully can put away the revolver anytime she chooses and move on" (Gallo, 2001, para. 5).

CHAPTER VI

NEGOTIATING A CELEBRITY ROLE MODEL

Negotiation Processes of Gillian Anderson

There was a time when I started reading the letters and people were saying, "You saved my life," or interviewers would say that Scully was a role model for young women. It stroked my ego for about five minutes before I thought, I don't know if I can handle this. I always felt that they were talking about Scully; it had nothing to do with me. But the more I started to talk about her character traits – how honest she was, how passionate about doing the right thing – the more I took cues from the way she handled herself (Gillian Anderson in Flaherty, 2002, Success section, para. 3).

In determining the best way to address the question of how Gillian Anderson negotiates her position of role model, it became apparent that inquiry would need to begin at a higher level. Fundamentally, Gillian Anderson's status as role model emanates from her primary position of star. How she negotiates the demands and limits of the star system has direct implications for how she manages being a role model. Gillian Anderson did not set out to be a cultural icon. Rather, the fact that Scully was a groundbreaking character in terms of television women is what instantly accorded Gillian Anderson authority as a woman to be emulated. Her role model status is a product of her celebrity status, both of which function within the larger context of stardom.

The major themes emerging from the data on Gillian Anderson reveal an ambivalent relationship between star and stardom, and an affinity between star and fans. The following analysis develops ideas on Gillian Anderson's star image, her use of celebrity privilege in social activism, the nature of her relationship with fans, what power she holds as a working actor, and the accrued benefits of playing Scully for nearly a decade. Gillian Anderson is quoted extensively throughout the discussion in an attempt to portray the scope of her negotiations within the broad realm of stardom and within her particular position of role model.

Star Image

As a bona fide Hollywood star, Gillian Anderson is somewhat atypical. In regard to the industry's expectation that she exude a certain star image, she explains, "I thought, 'I can't possibly hold this responsibility of dressing right in public, saying the right things, and having to think about how one projects oneself out there in the public.' I finally just said, 'I can't. That's not who I am'" (Gillian Anderson, personal interview, March 3, 2002). In describing how she feels about press junkets and self-promotion, she is even more explicit: "[T]hat aspect of it I absolutely despise" (Kimber, 2003, para. 7). Gillian Anderson's frustration with her mediated image stems from more than just wearing the proper attire at a Hollywood function or performing obligatory publicity in support of product; she is also dissatisfied with how she is portrayed in the popular press: "I can't tell you how many times I read about myself and, not only do I think, 'I did not say that in that way,' but sentences have been put elsewhere to mean something else. It's always about the angle. ... This is supposed to be so that the audience and public can get a little bit more about *who she is*, but it doesn't resemble me whatsoever" (Fischer, 2001, para. 8). This attitude is revealing in light of her being one of the most celebrated female stars of the 1990s and having received positive press support for nearly all her professional pursuits. Gillian Anderson sees the disconnect between her real self and what is offered for public consumption, innocuous though it may seem, as a threat to her authenticity. Her displeasure ultimately stems from the inability to retain some sort of power over her own image: "At the end of the day, you can have no f**king control. You can sit in front of somebody and think that you are having an intelligent conversation, and yet they will print what they want" (Kimber, 2003, para. 5).

By sharing publicly her discontent with the imposed conditions and manipulations of stardom, Gillian Anderson actually works to reinforce her legitimacy as a celebrity idol. The "indubitable sincerity and authenticity" (Dyer, 1986, p. 11) with which she reveals herself provides a glimpse into the *real* Gillian Anderson, what Dyer contends is the privileged knowledge sought by fans. Her forthright comments about the entertainment industry and the press can be interpreted by admirers as courageous, especially given that the continuance of her career largely depends on the support of these two cultural institutions. Fans can be proud that Gillian Anderson sets herself apart from mainstream Hollywood; that she is unique in resisting its manipulating control of her image. Gillian Anderson may be famous, but her outsider behavior conveys the sense that she is also "normal," and with that fans can identify.

Although Gillian Anderson flatly declares she is "not interested in being a movie star" ("Red-haired," 1998, para. 11), she does want to remain a working actor: "Acting is definitely the only reason I do what I do, because this is what feeds my soul and this other stuff is bullshit" (Fischer, 2001, para. 2). In order to be offered good roles and have opportunities to work with respected directors, Gillian Anderson – as actor *and* image – must remain a bankable commodity by industry standards. To that end, she does participate in press junkets, attend premieres, appear as a guest on talk shows, and "look" the part of a star: "Unfortunately, there is no way around it, and you have to realize that this is what I have to do" (Kimber, 2003, para.7). The ways in which Gillian Anderson negotiates stardom specific to star image – by airing her frustrations with the business while dutifully operating within its boundaries so that she may continue in the craft that she loves – work simultaneously to endear her to fans and keep her employed.

Social Activism and Celebrity Privilege

Social activism is another means by which Gillian Anderson negotiates her position within stardom, and which further provides an avenue for fan identification and role modeling. She has said that helping others is a way to cleanse herself of the trappings of Hollywood: "Maybe it just balances out all the icky other stuff. After the nine hours you've been sitting and talking about yourself...you want to go out and feed homeless people" ("Yahoo! Chat," 2001). Her efforts to make a difference in the lives of others have focused mainly on raising money for research into neurofibromatosis, a nervous disorder marked by tumor growth and which has been diagnosed in her younger brother. Second to her commitment to neurofibromatosis research, Gillian Anderson devotes time and money to the Buskaid Soweto String Project, an orchestra of teenage musicians from South Africa. She first became aware of Buskaid from hearing its director, Rosemary Nalden, featured on National Public Radio, who she immediately contacted with an offer to underwrite the group's touring expenses for a trip to Los Angeles. Gillian Anderson is also affiliated with the Feminist Majority Foundation (FMF), beginning in 1996 when she served as a spokesperson against passage of an anti-affirmative action initiative in California, and thereafter through regular involvement in FMF-sponsored events to support women's reproductive rights in the United States as well as assist women and girls in Afghanistan. Information about and links to each of these wholly dissimilar nonprofit organizations are provided on the Official Gillian Anderson Website.

What this selective participation in charities and social causes suggests about Gillian Anderson is that, if she must succumb to the "icky" side of celebrity, then she does so with a corresponding effort to use celebrity to her advantage: "The highlight of being a celebrity for me is it gives one a platform for having a voice for issues that one considers to be important. I've been able to speak out on many issues that are important to me and, as a result of that, there's been a large contingent of fans that have got involved in these issues and have gone on to get involved in things that are important to them" ("BBC Chat," 2002). It is at this point, where Gillian Anderson uses the privilege and power afforded her by fame to bring attention to larger issues, that an understanding of how she negotiates her position as a role model to fans begins to take shape.

Gillian Anderson became involved in social issues so as to make a difference in effecting change and, in fact, was motivated to a degree by Scully: "As I started doing interviews and talking about the intelligence and the compassion and her pursuit of justice, I started to think: 'Am I that person? Can I live up to that? Are there things that I need to shift about the way I operate in the world?'" (personal interview, March 3, 2002). After working steadily on *The X-Files* for about two years and being necessarily self-absorbed as she balanced an exhausting taping schedule, marriage, and motherhood, she recalls, "I picked my head up out of the sand and looked around and thought, 'Oh, wait a minute, there's people out there. There are things that need to be said and done.'" (personal interview, March 3, 2002). Gillian Anderson's heightened sense of social conscience that emerged during the third season of *The X-Files* coincided with an increasing awareness of her role model status apart from the Scully character. Naturally, she had known since the first season (1993-94) that Scully was lauded as a new kind of television female role model, and had even attempted to incorporate certain aspects of Scully into her own identity, but it wasn't until 1996 when she came to comprehend that she, too, was regarded as a celebrity role model (personal interview, March 3, 2002).

The confluence of Gillian Anderson's interest in social activism, mounting public expectations of herself as role model, and continuing popularity of Scully as role model created an ideal opportunity for her to exercise some control over her mediated star image and, at the same time, help others: "I started to realize that I could have some influence on money being raised and consciousness being expanded" (personal interview, March 3, 2002). Since then, she has constructively used her celebrity image to bring money and awareness to favored charities and social issues. The attention she pays such entities has been reproduced in some admiring fans who, wanting to pay homage to their role model, embrace her altruistic interests as their own to the extent that they raise money for her preferred causes. In addition to what personal satisfaction Gillian Anderson experiences in her work on behalf of others, the various organizations she publicly supports further profit by way of fan contributions and participation. Fans, likewise, have benefited by role modeling Gillian Anderson's efforts to foster the advancement of certain social issues, leading some to become involved in their own local communities.

Relationship with Fans

Just as maintaining her star image is challenging at times for Gillian Anderson, so too is maintaining her role model image. Specific to fans' reverence for her as role model, she occasionally feels overwhelmed by the responsibility to be perfect, declaring, "You know what? They have no idea. They have no idea!" (personal interview, March 3, 2002). Fans are demanding of their idols, and sometimes have unattainable expectations about how stars should behave. In regard to how she manages such expectations, Gillian Anderson employs different methods depending on her prevailing state of mind, one of which involves doing nothing: "I stay quiet for periods of time...where I need to hibernate from it, and those are times when I feel that I have nothing to say. [I] just keep my mouth shut and concentrate on storing and then building up my strength again – strength in terms of emotional and physical and physiological strength" (personal interview, March 3, 2002). When she does have something to say to fans, one way is by responding to questions submitted through the Official Gillian Anderson Website in a regular feature called Question of the Month. Part of her negotiation of being a role model entails bonding with fans, which she accomplishes through candid communication. The following excerpt from the June 2003 Question of the Month reflects the straightforward rapport Gillian Anderson maintains with her fans:

> Oh, by the way, there seems to be a lot of complaints about the fact that I should get off my ass and work already. Well, for those task masters amongst you, you will be happy to know that before the end of the year I will be doing one and maybe even two films and neither of them is My Scorpion Soul, for crying out loud. You will be filled in with details once they are confirmed but, in the meantime, keep your knickers on! I have been living my life for once in nine years and I am having a fantastic time of it and I deserve to take as long as I damn well please before jumping into the grind of the business again. ... Life is just too short and there is so much to do and so much to see. But other than that, thanks for your support. Tee hee. Enough. –me ("Question of the Month," 2003).

This virtual venue for directed dialogue with fans, in addition to online chats and other public events where her words are transcribed verbatim and posted on the Internet, allows Gillian Anderson the authenticity she is denied by the popular press. By circumventing the Hollywood publicity machine and going directly to her fans, she ensures that people who most admire her can see the Gillian Anderson that *she* offers for public consumption.

Because she has been labeled a role model since the dawn of her celebrity in 1993, Gillian Anderson has spent nearly her entire professional career negotiating the ramifications of this esteemed position. Initially, she was not overly sympathetic toward her fans' collective desire to know her and be known by her. Her attitude of aloofness shifted, however, at the beginning of *The X-Files'* second season when fans from around the world sent her handmade gifts of congratulations on the birth of her daughter: "It showed me another aspect of fans that I hadn't been aware of before – that's based more in appreciation and love than in annoying neediness" (Anderson, 2000, para. 25). This enhanced discernment of fans soon led to a personal sense of responsibility and an equivalent sense of inadequacy at meeting their expectations. She eventually learned how to balance her relationship with fans in part by embracing her position of role model. The copious correspondence Gillian Anderson received over the years on her virtues as a role model has afforded her unique perspective on fan motivations and practices as well as the lessons she hopes are learned through each person's fan experience:

> Every thought that they have about Scully or about Gillian to use initially for their own strength is fantastic, if that's how it can be used. But the important, essential next step is for them to then find where that resonates in their own bodies, and to draw on that which exists in themselves and not continue to think of me or the character in order to get up out of bed in the morning. If it can be an impetus and a starting point, then that can be incredibly healthy and a great guideline; but there needs to be a transition. I think that for any fan of a role model, the important thing to learn is that they are responding to those aspects because they exist within oneself already. It is important to then find that which exists within oneself, and not use the fantasy of the role model as a crutch (personal interview, March 3, 2002).

This insightful summation by Gillian Anderson on how role models should ideally function in people's lives aligns perfectly with Caughey's (1984) theory on the reasons fans choose to follow certain stars over others: "The appeal is often complex, but the admired figure is typically felt to have qualities that the person senses in himself but desires to develop further. The admired figure represents an ideal self-image" (p. 54). Gillian Anderson's aspiration for fans is that they not be satisfied with emulating her or Scully, but that they learn to look inward to discover and develop their own positive qualities toward greater personal growth. She and Scully are useful only insofar as they can motivate movement in that direction.

Authority of the Actor

Gillian Anderson's status as role model is founded on more than a connection to Scully and a predilection for causes and fans; it is also based on how she negotiates elements of her occupation. Within her privileged realm of role model, she is respected enormously. Yet, as a working actor in Hollywood, her authority is elusive. A discussion about Gillian Anderson's professional circumstances is warranted here in order to illuminate the differences between her distinguished cultural position as role model to women and her personal experience as a contemporary career woman.

It was clear to producers early on that Gillian Anderson was a vital component to success of The X-Files. Network executives' initial concerns over whether viewers would find her attractive enough quickly dissipated in light of positive fan feedback and rapid ratings growth, which were bolstered by select popular press reviews that went so far to proclaim her "the glue that holds *The X-Files* together" (Strachan, 1995, para. 7). Gillian Anderson was certainly valued for her acting ability and popular appeal, but any contribution to the series she might offer regarding story ideas or character development for Scully was routinely disregarded: "I have very little involvement in her future paths at all. That's really something that they have total control over, and I may make suggestions now and again about thoughts that I may have about her path. But most of the time they ignore me!" (Lambert, 1998). Executive producer Chris Carter maintained complete authority over stories and characters throughout the run of the series, disallowing any departure from his own creative vision, as explained by Gillian Anderson during the first season: "[Chris Carter] has strict guidelines about who she is, and he's pretty determined to keep her within those guidelines" (Durden, 1994, para. 16). And repeated eight years later during the last season: "Chris has been pretty good from the beginning in trying to figure out exactly what...needs to be told in terms of all the characters. You can't fight Chris" ("Free Agent," 2002, para. 15). Still, Carter's insistence that Scully remain so staunchly skeptical in the face of obvious paranormal indicators made Gillian Anderson uncomfortable about how she and the character might be perceived: "It's hard to keep being the skeptic. I've had this conversation a couple of times with Chris Carter, where I've just said, 'I have a feeling that the audience is laughing at me because I'm saying essentially the same stuff over and over again'" (Lipsky, 1997, para. 11). His customary reply was that she was a doctor and a scientist and would therefore always be skeptical. Rebuffed in her request to Carter that Scully's standpoint be softened in response to the strange phenomena she (and the audience) observes, and realizing that her input would likely never be valued to the point of implementation, Gillian Anderson contented herself with attending to priorities in her personal life instead of fighting that which she could not change in her professional life: "I've focused my energy in other ways in my life and not really got involved in the process" ("Free Agent," 2002, para. 15).

Her authority to impose changes on Scully through dialogue and narrative may have been clearly restricted, but what she did have under her control was the ability to make adjustments to the character through the code of acting. In the same vein that Scully's principles positively influenced Gillian Anderson, Gillian Anderson likewise infused Scully with traits of her own: "I think Scully has become more me over the years. At some point, I let the character go to the wayside more and let myself come in a bit more" ("Yahoo! Chat," 2001). This subtle shift is illustrative of a pattern Marshall (1997) believes is paramount to the continued viability of television programs: "Over time, there is a convergence of the star's personality with the character portrayed. The resource for new developments within the serial draws on the psychological deepening of the lead character through the personality of the star" (p. 130). Although what Gillian Anderson achieved in respect to her nuanced portrayal of Scully is not particularly uncommon for an actor, her actions take on greater significance when placed in context of Carter's obsessive control over his characters. Whether this convergence was intended by the star, permitted by the producers, or expected by the network for the health of the show, the outcome is that Gillian Anderson was able to exercise some degree of power over her character and hence over her professional image.

Benefits to Being Scully

Dyer (1979) writes, "Although I find it hard to conceive of a star having no power in the decisions made about her/his image or performance, just how much power s/he had and how s/he exercised it has to be determined by looking at specific cases" (p. 153). During the series' seventh season, Gillian Anderson petitioned for and was given approval to write and direct her own episode – the ultimate expression of professional authority for an actor, and an ideal "specific case" to study in regard to the power exercised by Gillian Anderson. Having established that performance was the only mechanism by which Gillian Anderson could wield any form of limited control in *The X-Files*, a closer examination of her experience writing and directing the one momentous episode where she could surmount at least some limitations reveals that the authority she seeks is not for a greater voice in the direction of her character or the series, but for personal expression and professional growth.

When asked what it means to be the first (and, incidentally, the last) woman to work in the dual capacity of writer and director within the "very powerful boys club" ("TV Guide Chat," 2000) of *The X-Files*, she responds, "They would've caught hell if they didn't let me do this, and I just happened to be a woman" ("On the Set," 2000). Her reply is about being allowed the opportunity to direct the episode she wrote, but it could be further construed to reflect Gillian Anderson's determination to be granted the respect due her for playing Scully so successfully for so many years. David Duchovny had already been credited with writing or co-writing several episodes by now and Gillian Anderson's chance to do the same was overdue. It was important to her to challenge herself professionally beyond the familiar haven of acting and to obtain some experience as a writer and director before *The X-Files* ended and her best chance to do either was lost. Her episode, entitled "all things," originally aired on April 9, 2000 to an estimated audience of 12 million viewers.

Because "all things" is a product of Gillian Anderson, who by that time had played Scully for seven seasons, it would be reasonable to assume she wrote the episode in order to provide some interesting back story to her beloved character. Indeed, Mulder's background had always been the more developed of the two leads, especially since his younger sister's disappearance 20 years earlier provided the impetus for his work on the X-Files. It would certainly be appropriate, then, to learn something meaningful about Scully even at this late point in the series. But developing her alter ego was not Gillian Anderson's intent: "Essentially, I never really set about writing the script the way that I did in order to set up history for Scully. I never really thought it out that much" (personal interview, March 3, 2002). Instead, her reasons for writing "all things" were of a more personal nature: "I made this episode for myself, for many reasons. To see if I could do it, and as a vehicle to express some philosophies" ("TV Guide Chat," 2000). These philosophies are conveyed through a story of Scully as she considers the myriad paths in life which have led her to the present moment and whether she has chosen them well. The episode's message is, by paying attention to the signposts along the way and trusting oneself to make wise choices even about seemingly inconsequential details, it becomes clear there is an order to "all things" – an insight that brings Scully a sense of peace and a confidence that she is where she should be in life, working at the FBI alongside Mulder. Because Gillian Anderson herself purports to be a "seeker," she aptly imbues Scully's passage into deeper personal awareness with far more spiritualism than had previously been written into the character. So, even though character development was not an priority for "all things," it nonetheless was a fortunate byproduct of the narrative. But the point here is not to elaborate on the story of "all things," since it is not the story itself but the process of *making* the story that is most significant to Gillian Anderson and is one of the greatest benefits she has received from being Scully.

When Gillian Anderson embarked on her first major project to write and direct an *X-Files* episode, she was understandably apprehensive: "I was very nervous that I didn't know anything, until I started to work out my shot list and I realized that I knew a lot more than I thought I knew" ("TV Guide Chat," 2000). Through the process, she came to learn she had extensive (though, up until now, untapped) knowledge about the technical processes of making a television show as well as a particular aptitude for directing. Perhaps more importantly, she learned what it feels like to occupy a position of authority and that her capacity for creativity extended beyond the bounds of acting, as she explains when asked how the experience affected her professionally:

> It was an extraordinary experience for me. ... I realized that I had things to say, which was very empowering. To sit in a room of 20 people who are looking at me for answers and be able to have answers based on knowledge was powerful. To not get overwhelmed with patting myself on the back, but just going, 'Okay. Alright. This is interesting. I know what I'm talking about here, and maybe this is something that I need to pursue more. Look how much I am enjoying myself right now. Look how creative I am able to be at this time'" (personal interview, March 3, 2002).

The popular press agreed with Gillian Anderson's assessment of her creative abilities; one writer remarking, "her mystical story was a treat to the eyes, ears, mind and soul" (Steffan, 2000, para. 5). Gillian Anderson had never before written or directed, but, on account of her being Scully, she was granted the chance to do both. She was furthermore able to accomplish this feat in a familiar environment surrounded by supportive colleagues, which increased her success and her satisfaction.

Considering Gillian Anderson's degree of influence was usually restricted in terms of all other *X-Files* plotlines, she nonetheless commands a healthy dose of respect by Hollywood standards: "Because of the fact that I have played this very intelligent, very strong character, I have a certain amount of authority as an actress" (Kimber, 2003, para. 10). In addition to the professional gains she has enjoyed by playing Scully (foremost which is writing and directing "all things"), she acknowledges there has also been great personal benefits. She is especially grateful for her role in establishing such a groundbreaking character as Scully: "She is a rarity. I'm very lucky to have the opportunity to play somebody, and for such a long time, that I like and respect, who is a step forward in the realm of television women" (Moore, 2000, p. 97).

Negotiation Processes of Female Fans

> Dear Gillian Anderson: As individuals, small groups, and large masses from all around the world, we have gathered together for 9 truly fabulous X-Files years. We have watched, we have cried, we have cheered, and we have come to believe. We will always cherish the many hours of entertainment and happiness your hard work, dedication, and kindness have allowed us to experience. You will always be remembered with much joy and affection. Today we say, in many different languages, what we all feel in unison – a very heartfelt THANK YOU! With gratitude, your fans ("*The X-Files* Special Farewell Edition," 2002).

The open letter above constitutes a paid advertisement in a special edition of the *Hollywood Reporter* published in tribute to *The X-Files* series on occasion of its final episode. As a thank you from fans worldwide to Gillian Anderson, it was funded through donations by over 200 people whose names were posted online by its organizers (indicating 85% female participants). The $4,000 in additional funds collected over actual cost of the ad was donated to one of Gillian Anderson's favorite organizations, the Buskaid Soweto String Project.

At this point in the analysis, the preceding quote provides a useful illustration to review the celebrity role model construct. This particular expression of appreciation for Gillian Anderson is symbolic of how individual components of the celebrity role modeling process coalesce to form an identifiable cultural construct. It includes elements of text, star, popular press, and fans, all of which are integral to the viability of such a construct. Beginning with text, the letter makes clear that it is on account of *The X-Files* and Scully that these fans have been inspired to watch, cry, and cheer in the course of their media consumption. Though it does not make specific reference to her as role model, the words "fabulous," "cherish," "affection," and "gratitude" strongly suggest that Scully is a much-loved character for viewers. Along with the fictional Scully, the real person of Gillian Anderson has also touched the lives of fans, garnering abiding respect for her hard work, dedication, and kindness. As for the popular press, the fact that fans use the forum of the *Hollywood Reporter* to publicize their esteem for Gillian Anderson demonstrates its significance. Rounding out the construct are the fans that made this ad possible.

Indeed, it is the fans who do much of the work, or negotiation, within the role model construct. And, while exploring the diverse negotiation and identification processes in which fans engage pertaining to Scully and Gillian Anderson would be extremely edifying, it would be an enormous undertaking. Therefore, by necessity, this analysis considers only a narrow aspect of fan identificatory practices – what some fans *say* about these two role models and, predominantly, what some fans *do* in honor of them, as can be gleaned from choice Internet postings. The analysis begins with a general outline on the process of role modeling as it applies to fans imitating celebrities.

Process of Celebrity Role Modeling

Although the process of celebrity role modeling necessarily varies depending on the individual fans involved and the idols they imitate, a natural path of progression can still be traced. It ordinarily begins with a media text, develops into fondness for a particular character, extends to knowledge about the real life star who plays that character, intensifies into an attachment to the star as role model, and culminates in behavior imitative of that role model. Critical theory on fandom holds that serious fans do not remain content with knowing merely the fictional side of their favored characters, but seek to learn about the actors who fulfill those roles. Fans' curiosity about the actual star behind the portrayal is usually prompted by a need to augment their circumscribed knowledge of what is presented in daily or weekly episodes with a more "expanded" version of their idol. Ferris (2001) describes the predictable transition from love for a character to admiration for her embodiment (which is oftentimes expressed in terms of love) as one where "the character identity recedes, and the actor's noncharacter identity comes into focus: he or she is a 'real' person whose everyday life involves work, home, and family, just like the reader's" (p. 31). Characters are inherently fictional beings that exist at the hand of writers and producers. They are predetermined entities operating within predetermined stories that, obviously, cannot literally interact with their admirers.

Conversely, actors are real life individuals that afford myriad points of attraction and interaction for their real life fans – they have the ability to be seen in public, sign autographs, respond to and ask questions of fans, lead interesting private lives, and pursue activities outside of acting – essentially serving as *authentic* objects of admiration with whom fans can identify.

The data collected on fans of Scully/Gillian Anderson support this general description of role modeling, but with the qualification that rarely are the boundaries between character and star distinct. Admiration for her/them oftentimes overlaps. What fans seem to ultimately identify with and strive to imitate, then, is a synthesis of Scully and Gillian Anderson. This concept was introduced in the preceding chapter relative to how the popular press has conflated of the image of Gillian Anderson with that of Scully. Tracing subtle distinctions between character and star based on which image fans identify as their "source of strength" is beyond the parameters of this component, though, and not pertinent to the overall discussion. For sake of simplicity, then, the real person of Gillian Anderson will primarily serve as the subject of discussion in illustrating the customary process of celebrity role modeling as well as in the ensuing analysis on fan identificatory practices.

Gillian Anderson first entered popular culture consciousness by way of *The X-Files*. Having appeared in only one episode of a short-lived teen television series and in one B-movie, very few people had ever seen her prior to debut of the show in 1993. This is significant in that the process undergone by fans who role model Gillian Anderson began not with Gillian Anderson, or even with Scully, but with *The X-Files*. Viewers who ultimately became dedicated fans of Gillian Anderson started on their path to fandom through an initial attraction to the televisual text. Whether instantaneously or over the course of months or even years, the pleasure these prospective fans derived from the series progressed into attachment to the Scully character, which eventually led to affection for the star herself. With Scully being the groundbreaking character she is in regard to television roles for women, it is not unreasonable that many female viewers find her appealing. The intelligence, confidence, and compassion she exudes are all desirable qualities that most people would aspire to. Gillian Anderson similarly exhibits enviable characteristics, including a proclivity for frankness and sensitivity to socially marginalized groups. The purpose in mentioning these attributes of Scully and Gillian Anderson is to convey that, somewhere amid the diverse personality traits of these two images, female fans are bound to recognize at least some aspect of themselves. Upon seeing an ideal embodiment of traits they value, and recognizing their own potential for improvement, fans enter into what Stacey (1994) calls a "dialectical interplay" (p. 227) between self-image and screen image toward adapting their identities to be more closely aligned with the ideal woman before them. This negotiation process can entail imitating facets of the admired star that range from attitude to activism.

Transforming Attitude

In reading online message boards dedicated to Gillian Anderson, it is apparent that fans want her and other fans to know that she has transformed their lives. This sentiment is most commonly expressed in references to being inspired by Scully and/or Gillian Anderson to cope with life and to grow as individuals. Details about the process are generally not provided, with postings conveying information mostly insofar that fans are somehow "better" for imitating their role model, as demonstrated in a post declaring, "I do think that Gillian Anderson has played a historical part in changing...a significant and forever unknown number of women out there such as myself who have bettered themselves in some way as a direct result of the strength they drew from this actress and character." Even when unable to articulate precisely how they have been personally affected by Gillian Anderson, these fans still credit her with positively influencing their attitude.

These changes in attitude take many forms. For example, the fact that Gillian Anderson merely exists and moreover communicates in an open and honest manner with her fans through the Question of the Month forum is enough to provoke a sense of joy in one woman's outlook on life: "I read her beautiful words just before I stepped out the door. I have to say how wonderful the world appeared to me after feeling such warmth coming off my computer screen. I found myself smiling at everyone on the bus, and I don't care if they thought I was nuts, because I was so incredibly happy to be alive." By her own account, Gillian Anderson was instrumental in altering this woman's behavior. Her blissful reaction to what she read may have lasted throughout the week or only for this one day, but her state of being was at least transformed for a time, sufficiently so that she posted publicly about her experience. Because this particular fan does not make mention of her attitude prior to reading what Gillian Anderson wrote, it can reasonably be assumed that she felt fine to begin with and felt even better after hearing from her role model.

Along with serving as a source of joy for some fans, Gillian Anderson is most often cited as a source of inspiration. Fans commonly express transformations in attitude that are rooted in a desire to be more like her, such as in instances where her conduct inspires them to continue in spite of the challenges that confront them in life. In sharing why she admires Gillian Anderson, a woman reveals, "Sometimes, when my routine, my never ending working hours, my headaches make me feel miserable, I try to remember her little gestures of kindness, her strength, the way she struggles with her limits, and I myself am inspired to go on too." The encouragement this fan receives from Gillian Anderson is probably not as outwardly apparent as it is internally restorative. She has observed Gillian Anderson enough to know that even celebrities such as her idol can encounter hardship in life, but can also remain kind and strong in the midst of their struggles. In following the good example set by her role model, she is able to persevere.

Occasionally, fans do post exactly how or why their attitude has been transformed for knowing Gillian Anderson, consequently providing valuable insight into her specific influence as a celebrity role model. One young fan drew upon Gillian Anderson's personal experience with divorce in order to manage her own pain in a similar situation: "For the past nine years, I've looked to you for strength. When you got divorced, my mom had just gotten divorced, too. I was so upset over it and I didn't know if I could make it and help my mom through. But when I saw you being so strong, I knew that I could make it too." The likelihood that this fan probably knew others who themselves or their parents had undergone divorce, yet chose instead to look to Gillian Anderson for strength, is indicative of the influential position that she (and many celebrities) play in contemporary culture.

As discussed herein, fans consult their role models for various reasons, sometimes to such an extent that "a deeper identification in which the media figure's values and plans are incorporated in the fan's social behavior" (Caughey, 1984, p. 59). Examined next is an example of the influence Gillian Anderson has had on the social activism of certain fans, conveniently introduced by one fan commenting on how her own life has been transformed: "So, to answer the question has Gillian inspired me? Yes, indirectly she has because I've seen some of her fans do some amazing things to raise money for different charity events as well as just volunteering their time, and it has inspired me to become involved."

Transforming Activity

On the subject of fan activity, Jenkins (1992) writes, "I am not claiming that there is anything particularly empowering about the texts fans embrace. I am, however, claiming that there is something empowering about what fans do with those texts in the process of assimilating them to the particulars of their lives" (p. 284). This "something" that fans *do* can take a variety of forms; in Jenkins' own study of *Star Trek* fans, it is the production and circulation within the fan community of cultural artifacts such as artwork and fan fiction. But there are also other avenues of activity for fans desiring a closer connection to the media texts and stars they admire; ways that draw upon organizational skills and monetary resources in lieu of artistic ability. For some Gillian Anderson fans, becoming involved in the same social causes that she supports constitutes an assimilation of her priorities into their own lives. That they initially have no other interest in neurofibromatosis or Buskaid is beside the point since their motivations stem from an attachment to Gillian Anderson, and not necessarily from what is relevant to their personal circumstances. Service is performed in honor of the admired figure. Regardless of initial motivation, there is an element of "empowerment" in the *doing* that service. Similar to Jenkins, Grossberg (1992) also addresses active fandom as being transformative in nature, asserting that it is "potentially enabling or empowering...for it makes it possible to move both within and beyond one's mattering maps" (p. 64). The fan who lends support is empowered and possibly transformed through her sense of doing good while the targeted organization and its constituency are most certainly empowered by the financial contributions received. Serendipitously, Gillian Anderson herself sums up this idea in advice given to teenage girls in the forward to *Girl Boss* (Kravetz, 1999): "Be of service. Whether you make yourself available to a friend or co-worker, or you make time every month to do volunteer work, there is nothing that harvests more of a feeling of empowerment than being of service to someone in need" (p. xi).

What follows is an examination of three cases where women, or groups consisting mostly of women, have been of service by organizing fundraising tributes to Gillian Anderson. The fundraisers were held to benefit Neurofibromatosis, Inc. and were largely arranged and executed via the Internet. The women are representative of a small set of extremely active fans whose behavior follows Stacey's (1994) definition of the extra-cinematic identificatory practice labeled "imitation." According to Stacey, imitation is "a partial taking on of some aspects of the star's identity" (p. 163) carried out "in relation to the desire for transformation of the spectator's identity" (p. 151). These fans want to somehow change themselves, supposedly for the better, and so look to their role model for ways to effect that change. Fans who dyed their hair red in honor of Scully could be said to have undergone a "transformation" of sorts. Here, the particular aspect of Gillian Anderson's identity taken on by fans entails advocating for her preferred social causes. Although some might argue that their efforts at showing appreciation for Gillian Anderson are not predicated on self-interest but rather on *her* preferences, it remains that in the process they still do "take on" those preferences as their own. If, and to what degree, these fans' own lives were personally transformed by their experiences is difficult to determine and would require interviewing to accomplish. Even so, the results of their efforts on behalf of Gillian Anderson, her charities, and other fans, have undoubtedly been transformative one way or another.

The "XFEOS Fundraiser Benefiting NF: In Honor of Gillian Anderson's Birthday" was held in 1998 and 1999 by a woman identified online as Dena. Organized through a now-defunct website, the fundraiser drew 19 contributors the first year and 31 the second year (approximately 85% female) from four countries, and collected a total of $726 which was forwarded to Gillian Anderson's mother, Rosemary Anderson, at the Neurofibromatosis Support Group of West Michigan. Dena's project was instigated at the open request of Gillian Anderson that, on occasion of her thirtieth birthday, fans wanting to express their appreciation do so by donating to a worthy cause in her name instead of sending gifts. Dena already maintained a website called The X-Files Episode Opinion Survey (XFEOS), and so used it to invite others to join in contributing to Gillian Anderson's most favored "worthy cause," Neurofibromatosis, Inc. (NF). To promote the endeavor, she enlisted fellow fans to help spread the word via their own websites or email, and added a section to the XFEOS site explaining how to become involved in the nonprofit NF organization. Dena explained online, "I wanted to do something different, something that will actually be noticed and will make a difference. This something is making a donation to NF in her name." In her bid to identify with her role model through affiliation with NF and Gillian Anderson's mother, Dena engaged in practices that "involve activities that are perceivable to others, and indeed often rely on the participation of others" (Stacey, 1994, p. 137). Dena's website made her efforts public, and her personal correspondence with Rosemary Anderson made her knowable to Gillian Anderson's family. Additionally, Dena's identificatory practice of soliciting donations required the participation of others in the form of messengers and contributors. Writing on her webpage following the second and final fundraiser, "I would like to thank Gillian Anderson and her loving family for giving us a reason to do this and help others," she credits her role model as the inspiration for her service.

Considered next is the Order of the Blessed Saint Scully the Enigmatic (OBSSE), an online "abbey" founded in 1995 by three women for purposes of collectively worshipping Special Agent Dana Scully. At its peak, OBSSE had a membership of over 2,500 people from more than 30 countries, held scheduled chats twice weekly, and maintained an exclusive mailing list of approximately 600 subscribers (see Wakefield, 2001, for an insightful treatment of this predominately female electronic community). From 1999 to 2002, one of the missions of OBSSE included facilitating annual "Scully Marathon" fundraisers to benefit NF. While the main OBSSE website is currently inactive, Scully Marathons have continued through locally organized efforts. Compared with Dena's method of soliciting donations for NF by simply asking people to send money, the size and scope of the OBSSE membership provided for a widespread fundraising campaign. The Internet proved a powerful medium toward encouraging fans to coordinate local marathons and in communicating where those marathons were being held in countries around the world. During the month of May, Neurofibromatosis Awareness Month, volunteer members hosted group marathons in dozens of cities that gathered *X-Files* fans together to watch continuously anywhere from ten to 13 predetermined "Scully-centric" episodes. Marathoners collected money from sponsors or made personal donations for the privilege of participation. OBSSE also sold Scully Marathon t-shirts, coffee mugs, and mouse pads.

As of 2002, the marathons had raised over $150,000, with all proceeds going to Neurofibromatosis, Inc. in the United States in addition to international NF organizations based in Australia, Brazil, Canada, France, Japan, the Netherlands, Portugal, and the United Kingdom. The OBSSE FAQ on Scully Marathons explains how this global phenomenon began: "Early in the history of the OBSSE the Order began to look for ways of expressing our thanks to Gillian Anderson for giving us such a wonderful character to 'worship' and for bringing us all together. We decided that donating to Gillian Anderson's favorite charity, NF, Inc., was the way to go about doing this." The results of these efforts, say the OBSSE coordinators, "have been beyond our wildest dreams." Over and above the funds raised to benefit NF, the Scully Marathons also afforded a venue for fans to become engaged in volunteer activity and to form new friendships in the process. Some even remained working with NF chapters, helping to design Christmas cards and stuff envelopes for charity events. As shared in the FAQ, "Everyone who has taken the time to meet and work with the people of the NF organization has felt rewarded by the experience."

The Official Gillian Anderson Website (GAWS) is the third case examined in regard to the extra-cinematic identificatory practice of fundraising performed by fans of Gillian Anderson in homage to their idol. Created in 1996 and still actively maintained, GAWS is sanctioned by Gillian Anderson to be her official website. As such, it operates to disseminate a variety of past and present information related to her personal and professional pursuits. In its early years, GAWS was maintained by a woman named Cynthia, who from 1997 to 2002 oversaw six increasingly successful online auctions raising money for NF. Following her departure in 2002, the 2003 auction experienced a significant drop in participation and thus donations; however, this was more likely due to the *X-Files* series ending than it was to a change in the website's ownership.

As far as Gillian Anderson fans advocating on behalf of her favorite charity, a great deal of credit is due Cynthia's work on GAWS. Administered primarily by one woman, but under the auspices of an extensive and authoritative online entity, the auctions fall somewhere between that of an individual endeavor (e.g., Dena) and a cooperative enterprise (e.g., OBSSE). With reasons similar to those set forth by Dena as to why she began fundraising, Cynthia explains, "In doing the website I found that everyone wanted to send Gillian something. I figured she probably had so many gifts from birthdays and other things that she would probably rather have her fans donate to her charity in her name. So I said, let's auction off signed Gillian stuff, and we hit a gold mine" (Causer, 2002, para. 4). What began as a small email auction of basic *X-Files* memorabilia and autographed photos eventually grew into a massive Yahoo!Auction affair that included items promising personal contact with Gillian Anderson such as a day-long visit to *The X-Files* set as her special guest (which sold for $17,000 in 2001).

As with OBSSE, Cynthia through GAWS drew upon many volunteers for support of the annual May event. She was also backed by Neurofibromatosis, Inc., which provided the letterhead for soliciting items to be auctioned; tracked donated items, contributors, sponsors, and winning bidders; paid postage for items mailed to winners; provided receipts; and followed-up with thank you letters to all participants. Even with this assistance, however, Cynthia still carried out the bulk of the work in her capacity as "webmistress" of GAWS. Managing all the items up for auction (at times numbering over 700) entailed storing them in her home, dividing and cataloging items according to type, uploading digital photos and writing descriptions for each one, regularly updating the website with bid information, responding to inquiries from potential contributors and bidders, coordinating money sent in by winning bidders, packaging and mailing the items, and recapping all that was done and won once it was over. Not long thereafter, Cynthia would begin another round of appeals for items to be auctioned the following year. As of 2004, the GAWS auctions had raised over $670,000 for NF.

Elaborating on the identificatory practices of fans, Jackie Stacey (1994) writes, "[I]dentifications do not take place exclusively within the imagination, but also occur at the level of cultural activity" (p. 171). Considering the breadth of the dedicated ventures undertaken by the women examined above, "cultural activity" may seem an understatement. This is particularly evident given that Stacey's own description of practices involving "actual imitation of a star" (p. 161) is limited to examples of replicating singing, dancing, and gesturing. Her complex schema stops short of considering practices that extend beyond personal activity and into social activism, like those demonstrated here. Gillian Anderson fans have clearly established that imitative role modeling encompasses practices having far greater influence and transformative potential than allowed for by Stacey.

In the course of imitating and honoring their role model Gillian Anderson, by 2004 OBSSE, Cynthia/GAWS, and Dena raised approximately $825,000 via online philanthropic campaigns for Neurofibromatosis organizations worldwide. OBSSE's grassroots method of fundraising fostered a widespread cooperative campaign that has resulted in the continuation of Scully Marathons in some countries even years after *The X-Files* series came to an end. GAWS, on account of its official status, enjoyed benefits brought by the full endorsement of Gillian Anderson, foremost being its ability to acquire for auction items highly valued by fans. Lastly is Dena, whose two campaigns were modest in nature compared with the multiple-year powerhouse operations of OBSSE and GAWS, but who probably serves as the best example of the social benefits that accrue from just one individual woman actively imitating her celebrity role model. She, alone, worked to raise over $700 for charity on behalf of Gillian Anderson.

CHAPTER VII

CONCLUSION

The celebrity role model construct – comprised of text, context, star, and fans – can be an incredibly powerful cultural force when its individual components form one cohesive concept. Presented in this examination of the two primary women of *The X-Files*, Agent Scully and Gillian Anderson, is a media text that depicts its lead character as a role model, a popular press that celebrates her character and attendant star as role models, a star that embraces her position as a role model, and female fans that aspire to imitate her/them as role model(s). Although the terms "role model" and "positive image" may have fallen out of favor among feminist cultural studies scholars, they are still invoked repeatedly by the press, celebrities, and fans in regard to fictional characters such as Scully. It is therefore prudent to conclude that feminist-inflected role model research of popular culture female images, particularly positive ones, is a valid and pressing pursuit.

In addition to demonstrating the efficacy of role model research in contemporary feminist media studies, this analysis also fills a gap in scholarship on *The X-Files*. Of the substantial amount of material published on this celebrated media text, only a handful specifically examine the imaginary character of Scully and/or her actual counterpart, Gillian Anderson. Of those that do focus on the meanings and influence of these dual star images, the tendency is toward a textually-based ideological analysis that more often than not argues the need for active resistant reading. As shown in the foregoing analysis, women do not necessarily need to read Scully, nor Gillian Anderson, resistantly in order to locate positive aspects worthy of emulation. Reading the text closer to the surface, where most average viewers consume and interpret entertainment fare, reveals multiple ways in which Scully and Gillian Anderson serve as constructive role models for girls and women. From this higher-level perspective, fans can readily identify and selectively incorporate into their own evolving identities modes of behavior and attitude modeled by these two female figures.

The Chapter Five analysis of the televisual text and popular press discourse makes clear that Scully and Gillian Anderson are securely *framed* as role models through powerful mechanisms of popular culture. In *The X-Files* text, Scully is afforded a privileged voice of narrative authority, notable mainly because it is rare for women characters to be granted such direct agency. She is furthermore written as highly intelligent, confident, and honest – all admirable traits that are consistently confirmed by the text. As for the popular press, the examination shows it routinely touted the virtues of Scully and Gillian Anderson in its coverage of *The X-Files* and its stars. Reinforced by a subtle but persistent conflation of Gillian Anderson with Scully, popular press accounts of the former as a celebrity, social activist, and professional actor were frequent and affirmative. Press treatment of Gillian Anderson's charitable efforts and film acting success, along with its customary coverage of her celebrity appeal, together worked to frame her as a laudable woman.

Building on the descriptions of how Scully and Gillian Anderson are textually and popularly framed as role models, Chapter Six illustrates how the actor herself and certain engaged female fans *negotiate* their positions within the celebrity role model construct. Uncommon in academic offerings on popular culture is the voice of professionals in the entertainment industry, particularly actors. The attempt to remedy that deficiency here, by conducting a personal interview with Gillian Anderson and examining scores of others she has granted over a ten-year period, reveals that the role model construct relies significantly on active participation of the role model star. Gillian Anderson's personal involvement in encouraging and maintaining her fan base promotes the continuation of an interested and committed following as well as bolsters her own work on behalf of social cause and aid organizations. It is also important to recognize that Gillian Anderson does not exist exclusively for the pleasure of fans. She is a real woman who faces family and career challenges similar to many contemporary women, and who should be interpreted in light of the mundane realities of life alongside the glamorous perks of her profession.

As presented in this research endeavor, the processes of fan identification and imitation can extend beyond individual circumstances and into an engagement with larger social issues. Fans emulate role models primarily because they want to become more like the object of their admiration. In shaping their identities to reflect the positive attributes of their idols, the transformation is generally for the better.

Many fans are satisfied with putting on an air of self-assuredness exhibited by a favorite star, or with altering their way of talking to parallel her mode of conversation. Others seek to share their experience as fans through involvement in fan communities, perhaps by attending conventions or posting to online message boards dedicated to their role model. These types of fan activities form the basis of studies by Stacey (1994) and Jenkins (1992), respectively; however, neither treatment provides a theoretical space for fans who imitate role models to the extent that society at large benefits. The select fans of Gillian Anderson examined in Chapter Six demonstrate that, by adopting her preferred charities as their own and working to raise money for those organizations in her honor, social entities outside of fans themselves and of *The X-Files* altogether are rewarded. The phenomenon presented herein, of female fans engaging in identificatory practices that model a female star's philanthropic activity in service to other groups, usefully links the political impetus of feminism with practices of popular culture.

Further analysis of *The X-Files*, one that entails interviews conducted with both casual and committed female fans of the series and its leading women, could delve the depth of this connection between feminism and popular culture by charting a continuum of fan identificatory activity and indicators of its lasting influence. Because the show ended in 2002, knowledge gained from such a study would most certainly present different conclusions than if it were performed during the series' run. Nevertheless, online fan websites dedicated to Gillian Anderson still exist, keeping female fans engaged with each other and their role model. Another avenue of inquiry pertinent to *X-Files* and Scully/Gillian Anderson fans concerns the formation of real world friendships among these women that share a common bond. Specifically, a closer look into whether and to what degree the people who were most involved in coordinating and volunteering with online fundraisers for Neurofibromatosis, Inc. stay(ed) in contact with each other. Mailing list members affiliated with the Order of the Blessed Saint Scully the Enigmatic, which sponsored Scully Marathons in cities around the world, could prove helpful in illustrating how relationships initially based on an admired figure have evolved over several years and, moreover, if socially conscious activity remains an important aspect of their lifestyles.

When I embarked on this project, my intent was to analyze *The X-Files* from the standpoint that Scully's (female) voice is routinely undermined by the dominant values implicit in the text, and thus only reclaimed for womanhood through techniques of active resistant reading. Such an approach aligned with the majority of feminist media studies, particularly in regard to images of women and woman as image, and also with published scholarship on Scully and Gillian Anderson. However, during the process of researching online the actual words of women who watch *The X-Files*, I came to recognize that their (and my own) viewing experiences did not entirely support the assumptions and arguments presented by academic writers on the subject. Unable to reconcile these divergent perspectives, I transitioned my emphasis away from a focus on the ideological workings of the text and toward an exploration of the pleasures and power that the images of Scully and Gillian Anderson afford female fans. This analytical shift was based on the fact that nearly all of the accounts I found relative to Scully and Gillian Anderson attested to the exemplary cultural influence of these two celebrated women. Indeed, discovering the ways they serve as a positive force in the lives of everyday women convinced me to adopt a more pragmatic methodology in studying media texts.

On the essence of qualitative research, Thomas Lindlof (1995) writes, "prolonged engagement and gradual acquisition of knowledge favor an inductive model of inquiry. ...data slowly resolve into concepts and specific research propositions through the investigator's own increasing skill at understanding. It is only near the end of the project that one learns what it is all about" (p. 56). My own experience throughout this study parallels Lindlof's depiction of the process – the discussions and conclusions ultimately presented in this analysis came about through my conscious attempt to yield to the data, even when that necessitated shifts in direction. While I continue to believe that identifying and exposing elements of dominant ideology inherent in cultural products is imperative, for my own research I determined that the approach most applicable to women viewers of *The X-Files* and to women in general is one that provides a redemptive feminist reading of Scully and Gillian Anderson as role models. It is clear that components of the circulating popular discourse on *The X-Files* have already framed, negotiated, and rated Scully and Gillian Anderson as A+ images of women. Accordingly, it is incumbent upon feminist media scholars to critically examine this and other cultural texts in light of the female celebrity role model construct.

APPENDIX A

Interview Questions posed to Gillian Anderson on March 3, 2002

1. At what point in your life as a celebrity did you become involved in your chosen charities?

2. Now that *The X-Files* has ended and you have more time, how might you become more involved in the issues that are important to you?

3. When did you realize that you had come into your own as a role model, apart from the Scully character?

4. How has Scully been a role model for you?

5. How do you manage fans' expectations of you?

6. How has your fans' charity work, done on your behalf, affected your own activism?

7. How important was your episode, "all things," to both Scully personally and to you professionally?

BIBLIOGRAPHY

The 25 most influential people in America. (1997, April 21). *Time, 149*(16), 40-70.

The 50 most beautiful people in the world. (1997, May 12). *People magazine,* 141.

Abercrombie, Nicholas and Longhurst, Brian. (1998). *Audiences: A sociological theory of performance and imagination.* London: Sage.

Adato, Allison. (2000, April). Save the world awards. *George, 5*(3), 48-61.

Adato, Allison. (2000, June). Dern for the better. *George, 5*(5), 72-78. Retrieved July 20, 2001, from Academic Search Elite database.

Anderson, Gillian. (2000, March 26). The truth about David Duchovny. *USA Weekend.* Retrieved March 24, 2000, from http://www.usaweekend.com.

Austin, Gayle. (1990). *Feminist theories for dramatic criticism.* Ann Arbor: University of Michigan Press.

Avalos, George and Liedtke, Michael. (2000, November 4). Let's hope we can give thanks for series' eighth season. *Contra Costa Times,* Entertainment News. Retrieved March 14, 2001, from LexisNexis Academic database.

Badley, Linda. (2000). Scully hits the glass ceiling: Postmodernism, postfeminism, posthumanism, and *The X-Files.* In Helford, Elyce Rae (Ed.), *Fantasy girls: Gender in the new universe of science fiction and fantasy television* (pp. 61-90). Lanham, Maryland: Rowman and Littlefield.

Bandura, Albert. (1977). *Social learning theory.* New Jersey: Prentice Hall.

Barker, June. (1996, June). File under X, for excellent. *Foxtel.* Reprinted in Transcripts. Retrieved December 23, 2003, from the Official Gillian Anderson Website, http://gilliananderson.ws/transcripts/96_97/.

Barrett, Michèle. (1992). Words and things: Materialism and method in contemporary feminist analysis. In Barrett, Michèle and Philips, Anne (Eds.), *Destabilizing theory: Contemporary feminist debates* (pp. 201-219). Stanford, California: Stanford University Press.

BBC Chat. (2002, December 6). Gillian Anderson. *British Broadcasting Company.* Retrieved July 24, 2003, from http://www.bbc.co.uk.

Bellon, Joe. (1999). The strange discourse of *The X-Files*: What it is, what it does, and what is at stake. *Critical Studies in Mass Communication, 16,* 136-154.

Bertsch, Charlie. (1998). The personal is paranormal: Professional labor on *The X-Files*. *American Studies, 39*(2), 107-127.

Bowman, Rob (Director). (1998). *The X-Files: Fight the Future* [Motion picture]. United States: Twentieth Century Fox.

Bravo for Anderson. (2001, April 23). *People magazine,* 20.

Brunsdon, Charlotte. (1989). Text and audience. In Seiter, E., Brochers, H., Kreutzner, G., and Warth, E.M. (Eds.), *Remote control: Television, audiences and cultural power* (pp. 116-129). London: Routledge.

Brunsdon, C., D'Acci, J., and Spigel, L. (Eds.). (1997). *Feminist television criticism: A reader.* Oxford: Clarendon Press.

Butler, Jeremy G. (Ed.). (1991). Introduction. *Star texts: Image and performance in film and television* (pp. 7-16). Detroit, Michigan: Wayne State University Press.

Carmody, John. (1993, October 7). The TV Column. *The Washington Post,* p. C8. Retrieved June 24, 2000, from LexisNexis Academic database.

Carroll, Willard (Director). (1999). *Playing by Heart* [Motion picture]. United States: Miramax.

Carter, Chris (Executive Producer). (1993, September 10). The Pilot [Television series episode]. In *The X-Files.* Beverly Hills, California: FOX Broadcasting Company.

Carter, Chris (Executive Producer). (1996, October 4). Herrenvolk [Television series episode]. In *The X-Files.* Beverly Hills, California: FOX Broadcasting Company.

Carter, Chris (Executive Producer). (1997, February 9). Memento mori [Television series episode]. In *The X-Files.* Beverly Hills, California: FOX Broadcasting Company.

Carter, Chris (Executive Producer). (2000, April 9). all things [Television series episode]. In *The X-Files.* Beverly Hills, California: FOX Broadcasting Company.

Casimir, Jon. (1996, February 12). *The X-Files*: The truth is in here. *Sydney Morning Herald,* The Guide, p. 6. Retrieved April 9, 2004, from LexisNexis Academic database.

Caughey, John L. (1984). *Imaginary social worlds: A cultural approach.* Lincoln: University of Nebraska Press.

Causer, Craig. (2002, March 15). Fanboy fundraising: Online fan groups net cash. *Non-Profit Times.* Retrieved April 17, 2002, from http://www.nptimes.com.

Chelsom, Peter (Director). (1998). *The Mighty* [Motion picture]. United States: Miramax.

Corner, John. (1999). *Critical ideas in television studies.* Oxford: Clarendon Press.

Cravens, Jayne. (1999, July 5). Connecting humans: Fan-based online groups use the Internet to make a difference. *Coyote Communications.* Retrieved March 19, 2004, from http://www.coyotecom.com/culture/fans.html.

Curti, Lidia. (1998). *Female stories, female bodies: Narrative, identity and representation.* Washington Square: New York University Press.

D'Acci, Julie. (1994). *Defining women: Television and the case of Cagney & Lacey.* Chapel Hill: University of North Carolina Press.

Davies, Terence (Director). (2000). *The House of Mirth* [Motion picture]. United States: Columbia Tri-Star.

Demme, Jonathan (Director). (1991). *The Silence of the Lambs* [Motion picture]. United States: Orion.

Denton, Andrew. (1996, July). *Australian Rolling Stone Magazine.* Reprinted in Transcripts. Retrieved December 24, 2003, from the Official Gillian Anderson Website, http://gilliananderson.ws/transcripts/96_97/.

Doane, Mary Ann. (1982). Film and the masquerade: Theorizing the female spectator. *Screen, 23*(3/4), 74-87.

Durden, Douglas. (1994, March 19). Anderson surprised that fans find Dana Scully an inspiring role model. *Richmond Times-Dispatch.* Reprinted in Transcripts. Retrieved August 10, 2001, from the Official Gillian Anderson Website, http://gilliananderson.ws/transcripts/94_95/.

Dyer, Richard. (1979). *Stars.* London: British Film Institute.

Dyer, Richard. (1986). *Heavenly bodies: Film stars and society.* New York: St. Martin's Press.

Epstein, Dan. (2000). *20th Century Pop Culture.* Philadelphia, Pennsylvania: Chelsea House.

Erens, Patricia (Ed.). (1990). Introduction. *Issues in feminist film criticism* (pp. xv-xxvi). Bloomington: Indiana University Press.

Faludi, Susan. (1991). *Backlash: The undeclared war against American women.* New York: Crown.

Ferris, Kerry O. (2001). Through a glass, darkly: The dynamics of fan-celebrity encounters. *Symbolic Interaction, 24*(1), 25-47.

Fischer, Paul. (2001, February). X marks the spot as Anderson heads to the big screen. *Dark Horizons.* Reprinted in Transcripts. Retrieved December 24, 2003, from the Official Gillian Anderson Website, http://gilliananderson.ws/transcripts/01_04/.

Fiske, John. (1987). *Television culture.* London: Methuen.

Flaherty, Mike. (2002, May 17). Case closed. *Entertainment Weekly,* 36. Retrieved May 28, 2002, from LexisNexis Academic database.

Free Agent. (2002, August). *Dreamwatch, 95.* Reprinted in Transcripts. Retrieved December 24, 2003, from the Official Gillian Anderson Website, http://gilliananderson.ws/transcripts/01_04/.

Friedan, Betty. (1963). *The feminine mystique.* New York: Norton.

Gabler, Neal. (1998). *Life the movie: How entertainment conquered reality.* New York: Knopf.

Gallo, Bill. (2001, January 18). Reinventing Gillian. *Miami New Times,* Movies. Retrieved March 14, 2001, from LexisNexis Academic database.

Gledhill, Christine. (1988). Pleasurable negotiations. In Pribram, E. Deidre (Ed.), *Female spectators: Looking at film and television* (pp. 64-79). London: Verso.

Grahnke, Lon. (1993, September 10). Fox's smart, spooky *X-Files* worth looking into. *Chicago Sun-Times,* Weekend Plus, p. 61. Retrieved June 24, 2000, from LexisNexis Academic database.

Great Expectations. (1999, August). *UK Cable Guide.* Reprinted in Transcripts. Retrieved December 24, 2003, from the Official Gillian Anderson Website, http://gilliananderson.ws/transcripts/99_00/.

Gross, Terry and Miller, Danny (Co-Executive Producers), and Shorrock, Roberta (Director). (2001, March 1). *Fresh Air* [Radio Program]. Retrieved April 12, 2002, from http://freshair.npr.org.

Grossberg, Josh. (2001, November 7). *X-Files* sequel definitely out there. *E! Online*. Retrieved November 8, 2001, from http://www.eonline.com.

Grossberg, Lawrence. (1992). Is there a fan in the house?: The affective sensibility of fandom. In Lewis, Lisa A. (Ed.), *The adoring audience: Fan culture and popular media* (pp. 50-65). London: Routledge.

Grossberger, Lewis. (1995, March 13). The zzzzz files. *MediaWeek, 5*(11), 30. Retrieved June 26, 2000, from Expanded Academic ASAP database.

Hall, Stuart. (1980). Encoding/Decoding. In Hall, S., Hobson, D., Lowe, A., and Willis, P. (Eds.), *Culture, media, language: Working papers in cultural studies, 1972-79* (pp. 128-138). London: Hutchison.

Handel, Leo A. (1950). *Hollywood looks at its audience: A report of film audience research*. Urbana: University of Illinois Press.

Haskell, Molly. (1974). *From reverence to rape: The treatment of women in the movies*. New York: Holt, Rinehart and Winston.

Horton, Donald and Wohl, R. Richard. (1956). Mass communication and para-social interaction: Observations on intimacy at a distance. *Psychiatry, 19*(3), 215-229.

Inness, Sherrie A. (1999). *Tough girls: Women warriors and wonder women in popular culture*. Philadelphia: University of Pennsylvania Press.

Jackson, Stevi and Jones, Jackie (Eds.). (1998). Thinking for ourselves: An introduction to feminist theorizing. *Contemporary feminist theories* (pp. 1-11). Washington Square, New York: New York University Press.

Jenkins, Henry. (1992). *Textual poachers: Television fans and participatory culture*. New York: Routledge.

Jensen, Joli. (1992). Fandom as pathology. In Lewis, Lisa A. (Ed.), *The adoring audience: Fan culture and popular media* (pp. 9-29). London: Routledge.

Jones, Alan. (2000, July). House of mirth. *Film Review, 595*.

Kantrowitz, Barbara and Rogers, Adam. (1994, December 5). The Truth is X-ed out there. *Newsweek*, 66. Retrieved June 24, 2000, from LexisNexis Academic database.

Kellner, Douglas. (1999). *The X-Files* and the aesthetics and politics of postmodern pop. *The Journal of Aesthetics and Art Criticism, 57*(2), 161-175.

Kimber, Richard. (2003, February 6). The X factor. *The Cambridge Student Newspaper*. Reprinted in Transcripts. Retrieved December 23, 2003, from the Official Gillian Anderson Website, http://gilliananderson.ws/transcripts/01_04/.

Kravetz, Stacey. (1999). *Girl boss: Running the show like the big chicks*. Chicago, Illinois: Girl Press.

Lambert, Sara. (1998, March). Irresistible. *Xpose Special, 4*. Reprinted in Transcripts. Retrieved August 10, 2001, from the Official Gillian Anderson Website, http://gilliananderson.ws/transcripts/98/.

Lavery, D., Hague, A., and Cartwright, M. (Eds.). (1996). *Deny all knowledge: Reading The X-Files*. Syracuse, New York: Syracuse University Press.

Leith, William. (1999, February 21). Space cadet. *The Observer*, Life, p. 14. Retrieved February 28, 2002, from LexisNexis Academic database.

Lewis, Lisa A. (Ed.). (1992). Introduction. *The adoring audience: Fan culture and popular media* (pp. 1-6). London: Routledge.

Lim, Dennis. (2000, December 12). Hothouse flower. *The Village Voice*. Retrieved December 10, 2002, from http://www.villagevoice.com.

Lindlof, Thomas R. (1995). *Qualitative communication research methods*. Thousand Oaks, California: Sage.

Lipsky, David. (1997, February 20). Her dark places. *Rolling Stone, 754*, 32-34. Retrieved July 20, 2001, from Academic Search Elite database.

Lowman, Rob. (2000, June 1). Creator Chris Carter looks forward to challenges of *X-Files* season. *Daily News of Los Angeles*. Retrieved June 3, 2000, from http://www.dailynews.com.

Lowry, Brian. (1995). *The truth is out there: The official guide to The X-Files*. New York: Harper Collins.

Markley, Robert. (1997, May). Alien assassinations: *The X-Files* and the paranoid structure of history. *Camera Obscura, 14*(40/41), 77-105.

Marshall, P. David. (1997). *Celebrity and power: Fame in contemporary culture*. Minneapolis: University of Minnesota Press.

McConnell, Frank. (1994, September 9). *The X-Files*. *Commonweal, 121*(15), 15-18. Retrieved June 26, 2000, from Expanded Academic ASAP database.

Melcombe, Lynne. (1995, October). Supernatural SuXXess. *BC Woman*. Reprinted in Transcripts. Retrieved August 10, 2001, from the Official Gillian Anderson Website, http://gilliananderson.ws/transcripts/94_95/.

Miller, Craig. (1994, August). An appointment with Dr. Scully: Gillian Anderson interviewed. *Wrapped in plastic, 12*. Reprinted in Transcripts. Retrieved August 10, 2001, from the Official Gillian Anderson Website, http://gilliananderson.ws/transcripts/94_95/.

Moore, Richard. (2000, July). The X-Woman. *Ultimate DVD, (7)*, 96-97.

Morrison, Mark. (2000, August). Sweet inspirations. *In Style*. Reprinted in Transcripts. Retrieved July 16, 2000, from the Official Gillian Anderson Website, http://gilliananderson.ws/transcripts/99_00/.

Mulvey, Laura. (1975). Visual pleasure and narrative cinema. *Screen, 16*(3), 6-18.

Mumford, Laura Stempel. (1998). Feminist theory and television studies. In Geraghty, Christine and Lusted, David (Eds.), *The television studies book* (pp. 114-130). New York: St. Martin's Press.

National Organization for Women Foundation. (2002). *Watch out, listen up!: 2002 Feminist Primetime Report* [Electronic version].

O'Hare, Kate. (2001, May 1). Anderson closes out her final X-File. *Zap2it*. Retrieved April 30, 2002, from http://tv.zap2it.com.

On the Set. (2000, March). *E! News Daily*. Reprinted in Headlines. Retrieved March 24, 2000, from Gilly.Net, http://www.gilly.net/headlines.html.

Parks, Lisa. (1996). Special agent or monstrosity?: Finding the feminine in *The X-Files*. In Lavery, D., Hague, A., and Cartwright, M. (Eds.), *Deny all knowledge: Reading The X-Files* (pp. 121-134). Syracuse, New York: Syracuse University Press.

Pennington, Gail. (1993, September 9). Science meets match in Fox's *X-Files*. *St. Louis Post-Dispatch*, Everyday magazine, p. 6G. Retrieved March 16, 2004, from LexisNexis Academic database.

Perenson, Melissa J. (2002, August). Scully's saga. *Sci-Fi magazine*. Reprinted in Transcripts. Retrieved December 24, 2003, from the Official Gillian Anderson Website, http://gilliananderson.ws/transcripts/01_04/.

Pollock, Griselda. (1977). What's wrong with images of women? *Screen Education, 24*, 25-33.

Question of the Month. (2003, June 26). *The Official Gillian Anderson Website.* Retrieved June 27, 2003, from http://gilliananderson.ws/inter/ questions.shtml.

Quill, Greg. (1993, August 29). Oddball *X-Files* pushes all the right buttons. *The Toronto Star*, p. D6. Retrieved June 24, 2000, from LexisNexis Academic database.

Red-haired *X-Files* sexbomb on a mission to make it in movies. (1998, September). *Empire magazine.* Reprinted in Transcripts. Retrieved July 16, 2000, from the Official Gillian Anderson Website, http://gilliananderson.ws/ transcripts/98/.

Rich, B. Ruby. (1990). In the name of feminist film criticism. In Erens, Patricia (Ed.), *Issues in feminist film criticism* (pp. 268-287). Bloomington: Indiana University Press. (Original work published 1978).

Rosen, Marjorie. (1973). *Popcorn venus: Women, movies and the American dream.* New York: Coward, McCann and Geoghegan.

Rowe, Kathleen. (1995). Studying *Roseanne.* In Skeggs, Beverly (Ed.), *Feminist cultural theory: Process and production* (pp. 46-61). New York: St. Martin's Press.

Saddy, Guy. (1997, March 13). *Flare.* Reprinted in Transcripts. Retrieved December 23, 2003, from the Official Gillian Anderson Website, http://gilliananderson.ws/transcripts/96_97/.

Schaefer, Stephen. (1998, June 14). The truth about Agent Scully. *The Boston Herald*, Arts and Life, p. 43. Retrieved June 24, 2000, from LexisNexis Academic database.

Schickel, Richard. (1985). *Intimate strangers: The culture of celebrity.* Garden City, New York: Doubleday.

Seiter, Ellen. (1999). *Television and new media audiences.* Oxford: Clarendon Press.

Shales, Tom. (1993, September 10). For the circular files. *The Washington Post*, p. G7. Retrieved June 24, 2000, from LexisNexis Academic database.

Simon says the science is in there. (1999, October 30). *The Boston Globe*, p. F2. Retrieved June 24, 2000, from LexisNexis Academic database.

Smith, Jack. (2000, September/October). High-powered performance.
Brntwd Magazine. Retrieved September 18, 2000, from
http://www.brntwdmagazine.com.

Spelling, Ian. (2000, June 17). *X-Files'* future rests with Scully: Duchovny signed on
for only half season. *The Ottawa Citizen*, p. K4. Retrieved April 9, 2004,
from LexisNexis Academic database.

Spelling, Ian. (2000, September). Requiem for a conspirator. *Starlog*. Reprinted in
Articles. Retrieved July 26, 2000, from Haven, http://idealists.simplenet.com/
articles/txfarts/starlog_sept_2000.html.

Stacey, Jackie. (1994). *Star gazing: Hollywood cinema and female spectatorship*.
London: Routledge.

Steffan, Janine Dallas. (2000, April 13). Seen, heard, said. *The Seattle Times*.
Retrieved April 14, 2000, from http://www.seattletimes.com.

Strachan, Alex. (1995, December 8). X marks the spot each Friday night. *The
Vancouver Sun*, p. C4. Retrieved June 24, 2000, from LexisNexis Academic
database.

Strauss, Bob. (1998, June 14). Anderson talks about her life on the Scully side. *The
Daily News of Los Angeles*, L.A. Life. Retrieved March 16, 2004, from
LexisNexis Academic database.

Strauss, Bob. (2001, February 18). Entering alien territory. *Star Tribune*, p. F6.
Retrieved March 14, 2001, from LexisNexis Academic database.

Surprise aura of success. (1994, February 18). *The San Francisco Chronicle*, TV
Commentary. Retrieved June 24, 2000, from LexisNexis Academic database.

Syson, Damon. (1996, October). 100 sexiest women in the world 1996. *FHM, 81*.

Thomas, Harry. (2001). Same old show, now Duchovny-free! *Rolling Stone*.
Reprinted in Rolling Stone Preview of Premier [Msg 1]. Message posted
October 31, 2001, to http://groups.google.com/groups?q=alt.tv.x-
files.analysis.

Thompson, Robert J. (1996). *Television's second golden age: From Hill Street
Blues to E.R.* New York: Continuum.

Thornham, Sue. (1997). *Passionate detachments: An introduction to feminist film
theory*. New York: Arnold.

Thornham, Sue. (1998). Feminist media and film theory. In Jackson, Stevi and
Jones, Jackie (Eds.), *Contemporary feminist theories* (pp. 213-231).
Washington Square, New York: New York University Press.

The truth is in here. (1999, June). *New woman*. Reprinted in Transcripts.
Retrieved December 23, 2003, from the Official Gillian Anderson Website,
http://gilliananderson.ws/transcripts/99_00/.

Tuchman, G., Daniels, A., and Benét, J. (Eds.). (1978). *Hearth and home: Images of
women in the mass media*. New York: Oxford University Press.

Tuchman, Gaye. (1978). The symbolic annihilation of women by the mass media. In
Tuchman, G., Daniels, A., and Benét, J. (Eds.), *Hearth and home: Images of
women in the mass media* (pp. 3-38). New York: Oxford University Press.

Tudor, Andrew. (1974). *Image and influence: Studies in the sociology of film*. New
York: St. Martin's Press.

Tulloch, John. (1990). *Television drama: Agency, audience, and myth*. London:
Routledge.

TV Guide Chat. (2000, April 7). Gillian Anderson. *TV Guide Online*. Retrieved
February 27, 2002, from http://www.tvguide.com.

van Zoonen, Liesbet. (1994). *Feminist media studies*. London: Sage.

Wakefield, Sarah R. (2001). Your sister in St. Scully: An electronic community of
female fans of *The X-Files*. *Journal of Popular Film and Television*, 29(3),
130-138.

Walker, James R. and Ferguson, Douglas A. (1998). *The broadcast television
industry*. Boston: Allyn and Bacon.

Walters, Suzanna Danuta. (1998). Sex, text, and context: (In) between feminism and
cultural studies. In Ferree, M., Lorber, J., and Hess, B. (Eds.), *Revisioning
gender* (pp. 222-257). Thousand Oaks, California: Sage.

Watkins, Craig S. and Emerson, Rana A. (2000). Feminist media criticism and
feminist media practices. *Annals of the American Academy of Political and
Social Sciences*, 571, 151-167. Retrieved March 14, 2001, from Academic
Search Elite database.

Westerfelhaus, Robert and Combs, Teresa A. (1998). Criminal investigations and
spiritual quests: *The X-Files* as an example of hegemonic concordance in a
mass-mediated society. *Journal of Communication Inquiry*, 22(2), 205-220.

Wilcox, Rhonda, and Williams, J.P. (1996). What do you think? *The X-Files,*
    liminality, and gender pleasure. In Lavery, D., Hague, A., and Cartwright, M.
    (Eds.), *Deny all knowledge: Reading The X-Files* (pp. 99-120). Syracuse,
    New York: Syracuse University Press.

Wild, David. (1996, May 16). *X-Files* undercover. *Rolling Stone, 734,* 38-44.
    Retrieved July 13, 2000, from Academic Search Elite database.

The X-Files meets the skeptics. (1997, January/February). *The Skeptical Inquirer,*
    21(1), 24-30.

The X-Files Special Farewell Edition. (2002, May 10). *The Hollywood Reporter.*

Yahoo! Chat. (2001, March 31). Gillian Anderson. Reprinted in Transcripts.
    Retrieved February 27, 2002, from the Official Gillian Anderson Website,
    http://gilliananderson.ws/transcripts/01_04/.

Wissenschaftlicher Buchverlag bietet

kostenfreie

Publikation

von

wissenschaftlichen Arbeiten

Diplomarbeiten, Magisterarbeiten, Master und Bachelor Theses
sowie Dissertationen, Habilitationen und wissenschaftliche Monographien

Sie verfügen über eine wissenschaftliche Abschlußarbeit zu aktuellen oder zeitlosen
Fragestellungen, die hohen inhaltlichen und formalen Ansprüchen genügt,
und haben **Interesse an einer honorarvergüteten Publikation**?

Dann senden Sie bitte erste Informationen über Ihre Arbeit per Email
an info@vdm-verlag.de. Unser Außenlektorat meldet sich umgehend bei Ihnen.

VDM Verlag Dr. Müller Aktiengesellschaft & Co. KG
Dudweiler Landstraße 125a
D - 66123 Saarbrücken

www.vdm-verlag.de

Lightning Source UK Ltd.
Milton Keynes UK
24 November 2009

146642UK00001B/250/P